The River Jordan

The River Jordan

By NELSON GLUECK

McGRAW-HILL BOOK COMPANY New York Toronto London Sydney

Library of Congress Catalog Card Number: 66-22910

23505

Additional illustration credits:

Government of Palestine, Department of Antiquities:
pages 52–53 (lower), 54–55, 56, 57, 58, 59 (right), 60–61, 62,
63 (lower), 66 (upper), 70 (upper), 72, 145 (right), 146, 157 (upper),
158–159, 160, 161 (upper), 164 (left), 165, 167 (lower)
American Schools of Oriental Research: pages 66 (lower), 167 (above), 168
S. J. Schweig: pages 50 (lower), 70 (lower), 71 (right)
The Matson Photo Service, Jerusalem: pages 49, 52–53 (upper), 63 (upper)
The Orient Press Photo Co.: page 68
Dr. Kathleen M. Kenyon: page 149
Keren Hayesod, Jerusalem: page 50 (upper)
Nelson Glueck: pages 65 (lower), 69

To my wife HELEN at whose request this book was written.

Contents

Herod Chart   217

Indexes

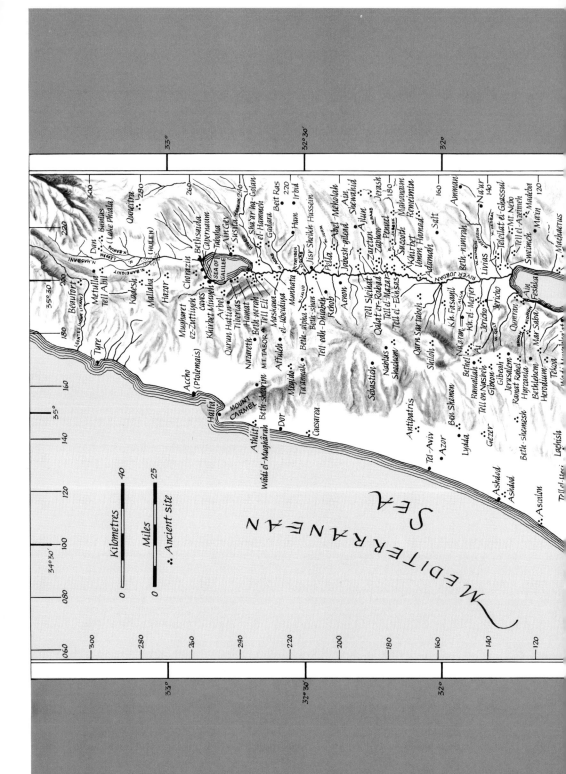

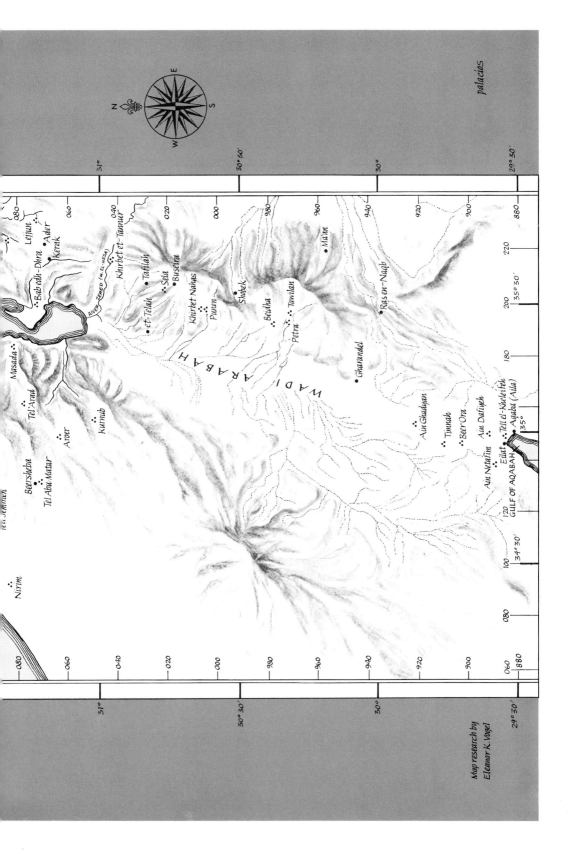

Map research by
Eleanor K. Vogel

Foreword

This is the story of the Jordan and its valley, formed after the disappearance of a very early prehistoric lake. The results of modern Biblical and archaeological research have been incorporated without stressing technical details and terminology. Some persons, incidents and sites have been highlighted to help portray the river's role in the pages of the Bible. Centrally located in world geography, the Jordan has left its mark on seventy thousand years and more of human history.

In the enigma of its influence, the Jordan is without compare. How can anyone assemble and properly interpret all the factors resulting in its enduring importance? There can, of course, be no final answer as to why Judaism and Christianity and their issue Islam developed along its banks and in adjacent lands and not elsewhere. These are matters that can be intensively contemplated and increasingly understood but never conclusively determined. And thus it is that we study and restudy the Jordan with astonishment and awe, because in connection with it, to use the language of religious experience, miracles were made manifest.

I am indebted to all those who helped make it possible for me, while director of the American School of Oriental Research in Jerusalem, to undertake the archaeological exploration particularly of the east side of the Jordan Valley. Especially helpful were Sir Alec S. Kirkbride, formerly British Resident in Transjordan, General John Bagot Glubb (el-Farik Glubb Pasha), for many years Officer Commanding the Arab Legion, and Mr. G. Lankester Harding, who was Chief Curator of Antiquities in Transjordan, now the Hashemite Kingdom of Jordan. My Archaeological Assistant, Mrs. Eleanor K. Vogel, has prepared the map, the Indexes and the Herodian Chart.

NELSON GLUECK

Hebrew Union College—Jewish Institute of Religion
Cincinnati, Ohio

The River Jordan

I / "To spy out the land"

(Numbers 13:17)

The geography of the Jordan

If an astronaut in his spaceship speeding high in the heavens were gazing down at the great fissure in the crust of the earth extending from northern Syria southward to the heart of Africa, he could observe in part of it the spiraling line of the Jordan River. Particularly noticeable would be the Sea of Galilee at the top, looking like an azure-blue jewel, and at the bottom the leaden gray pendant of the Sea of Salt, the Dead Sea. Still farther south he would behold the lunar landscape of the narrow empty wilderness of the Wadi Arabah, with its lower end touching the almost completely pent-up Gulf of Aqabah, one of the extended arms of the Red Sea. From the sources of the Jordan at the base of snow-capped Mount Hermon to the north shore of the Gulf of Aqabah is a straight line of only some 262 miles. Yet along this length much of the known story of the development of mankind can be traced.

The geography of the Jordan and Wadi Arabah Rift and the history of Israel are inextricably intertwined. The path of the Exodus led in part through the Wadi Arabah as far north as Punon (modern Feinan) on its east side. The character of the people of Israel had been formed by the time of their arrival there. Forty years of wandering in the wilderness had tested them to the marrow of their bones. Neither heat nor cold, hunger

1

nor thirst, weariness nor delay could divert them from pressing forward to the Promised Land, and coming back to it thereafter like homing pigeons whenever they were dispersed. Punon was for them a point of no return. There could be no retreat. It was onward or perish. They ascended thence to the top of the broken plateau above the east side of the Wadi Arabah, never faltering in their forward march until they reached the haven of their search.

Edomites and Moabites barred them from using the King's Highway that pointed like an arrow in the direction of their goal. This heightened their burden and lengthened their way, but did not confound them. Doggedly they detoured eastward through unfriendly terrain, till finally it became possible to turn westward and cross over the Jordan to the country of their covenant. Its passage assured them, little as they were aware of it, a permanent place in history. Physically and spiritually, the Jordan Valley and the Wadi Arabah became and remained the guideline of their destiny.

Burning off the mists of the past

The importance for Israel of the immense geological fault in which the Jordan Valley, the Dead Sea and the Wadi Arabah are contained can hardly be overestimated. Cisjordan and Transjordan were attached to it like wings to a body. It was both boundary and barrier between western and eastern Palestine, and the people on each side fought periodically with one another for its possession. Whoever controlled the rift in its entirety possessed the key to entire continents. It afforded security of passage to Syria, Arabia, Africa and India. The peaks of Israel's development as an independent kingdom coincided with the intervals of its mastery of the Jordan Rift. Of crucial value were the good water and soil of the Jordan Valley, the salts and bitumen of the Dead Sea and the minerals of the strategic roadway of the Wadi Arabah, with its seaport of Ezion-geber (Elath) providing unique access to international markets and enriching cultures.

Yet it was not very long ago that little was known about this strategic stretch of land between Mount Hermon and the Red Sea. Until well into the twentieth century of our era, it had largely been ignored by investigators and unintentionally maligned. The Wadi Arabah was dismissed as a useless wasteland. The Biblical information about it was either not sufficiently studied or believed in to enable it properly to be appreciated in geopolitical and historical perspective. The Jordan Valley received little scientific attention except for its cities of Beth-shan and Jericho. Even the erudite George Adam Smith assumed in his book *The Historical Geography of the Holy Land* that it "had never been populous," that most of the mounds in it were "probably the remains not of cities but of old brick fields," that towns had "always been few in the Valley" and that "it had deserved the name of Wilderness." The great historian Eduard Meyer believed that it was hopelessly barren, "burning hot between its mountain walls," and that irrigation agriculture had never been attempted there in pre-Roman times. And years later still, Arnold J. Toynbee disparaged the significance of the Jordan Valley for the story of civilization.

Four main reasons had been advanced for the supposed bleakness, emptiness and unimportance of the Jordan Valley fault—its intolerable heat, devastating malaria, savage animals and fiercely cruel nomadic inhabitants. The archaeological exploration of the Jordan Valley, made possible through advanced techniques and favorable political circumstances, has proved the incorrectness of these assertions. It is now possible to demonstrate that the Jordan Valley is of surpassing importance for the story of the evolution of mankind and the development of civilization. We now know that it was inhabited from early prehistoric times on and that there have been no major, permanent climatic changes there or anywhere in the Fertile Crescent during the last ten thousand years. Jericho was a highly developed city as early as about 8000 B.C. Everything that happened at Jericho and similar centers of habitation, for good or ill, is to be attributed not to radical shifts in weather but to the creative or destructive handiwork of man. Our new knowledge of ancient history is based primarily on archaeological findings.

Archaeology and the Bible

A book of theology

How does one go about discovering the locations and judging the nature of ancient settlements in regions sometimes scythed bare even of surface remains and which on occasion are actually plowed over and planted, as we found frequently to be the case in the Jordan Valley? What is the nature of the relationship between archaeological investigation and the understanding of history in the Bible? What are the tools and techniques of the trade?

First of all, it is extremely important for the explorer and archaeologist in Bible lands to pay careful attention to every bit of historical information and historical memory in the Bible. Whenever I have gone exploring in the Jordan Valley or the Wadi Arabah or in any part of Transjordan or the Negev, I have used the Bible as a guidebook of antiquity, giving wholehearted credence to its information, clues and even hints. My discovery and dating of King Solomon's copper mines, for instance, stemmed directly from belief in the essential correctness of the tantalizingly brief statement in Deuteronomy 8:9 about the presence of copper and iron in the Promised Land, and from utilizing every bit of information in the Bible about places and people mentioned in connection with these metals.

It needs to be underscored at the outset, however, that the proper evaluation of historical information in the Bible has no relevance whatsoever to the Bible's primary nature as an indescribably great book of theological belief and exposition. The methods and achievements of Biblical archaeology cannot be used to prove the concept of God in the Bible or its religious truths and ethical commandments. This is not the place, nor is it my purpose in this book, to dwell upon the infinite importance of the Bible as a whole, in whose insights and teachings I profoundly believe. Every book, every chapter, every page of the Bible is devoted in one way or another to expounding and emphasizing for the people of Israel and all mankind the existence and nature of God as the Source of all being, the Creator of the universe, the Father of all mankind, the God of history and humanity. The words of Sacred Writ echo above all else the unceasing dialogue between God and man.

For the exposition of their central and overriding thesis of the universality and omnipotence of God, who gave man the freedom to choose between good and evil, the editors of the Bible employed all kinds of literary materials. Among them were widely current myths carefully edited to suit their religious and didactic purposes. Well-known historical facts were selected from larger contexts to illustrate their a priori convictions. There were included also unvarnished biographical sketches of great folk heroes, whose shortcomings as well as virtues were highlighted to illustrate the consequences of injustice, the fragility of physical possessions and power, the strengths, potentialities and weaknesses of human beings, the perplexities, pains and pity of mortality, the meaning of real religion requiring translation into acts of justice and mercy and love, the necessity of humble acceptance, even without full understanding, of divine authority.

The authors of the Bible found God in the phenomena of nature and in the forces of history. In their contemplation of the hosts of the heavens, they were moved to wonder that God had concerned Himself with fallible human beings and particularly that He had endowed them with gifts making them little lower than angels. The faith of the Biblical writers was formidable. In their finest expressions they did not present the worship of God as being a paying proposition that would preclude the quirks of fortune, the suffering of the righteous, the abuse of the weak, the uncertainties and limitations of life. For them God was the Source of all being, whose ways were beyond comprehension, whose word was law, whose love was all-embracing, whose grace, mercy and lovingkindness were endless. It was in and through the Bible that they spelled out their understanding of God, the meaning of His mandates, the nature and condition of His relationship to individuals, Israel, the family of nations and all of mankind.

Historical source-book

Aware of the fact, then, that the Bible is first and foremost a religious document, we should nevertheless remember that it still makes copious use of selective historical materials. The Bible is our chief literary source of information about the early past of Israel and of peoples and cultures Israel encountered. The archaeological explorer can learn much by carefully considering both the broad scope and fragmentary accounts or even isolated details of historical information that the Bible provides in an illustrative and incidental fashion. It remains, nevertheless, often woefully deficient in the presentation of exhaustive historical materials.

As a matter of fact, the Biblical editors made no pretense of not being selective in their use of historical records or references. In effect they tell their readers, who might desire more details than are provided, to go to the same source materials from which they themselves culled their materials. "Are they not written in the Book of the Chronicles of the Kings of

Israel"? (I Kings 16:20). Or they refer to other basic records such as "the Book of the Kings of Judah and Israel" (II Chronicles 16:11), or the "Book of Jashar" (Joshua 10:13), or the "Book of the Acts of Solomon" (I Kings 11:41).

Unfortunately none of these documents has yet been discovered, and the chances of finding them are very poor unless they were sealed and stored in moistureproof places. Among recent fascinating discoveries of this type are the so-called Dead Sea Scrolls and the Nabataean legal documents found at Qumran and the nearby Wadi Murabbaat and the letters of Bar Kochba (Bar Kosiba) found at the Wadi Murabbaat, the Nahal Hever and Masada, overlooking or near the Dead Sea. There are also the epoch-making fourth-century-B.C. Samaritan papyri found in a cave in the Wadi Daliyeh a few miles north of Jericho. Archaeology comes into play, then, to fill lacunae in the historical information afforded by the Bible. All too often matters of obviously great importance can barely be gleaned from the Biblical records and frequently are lost in silence.

The purpose of Biblical archaeology

Much more archaeological investigation is required, for example, to fill out the picture of the Philistines that is only faintly drawn in the pages of the Bible. A beginning has been made at Ashdod, one of the Philistine cities mentioned in the Bible and known to have existed on the southwest coast of Palestine, but much more needs to be learned. These highly civilized sea-peoples from Crete (Caphtor in Amos 9:7) and other Aegean islands took advantage of the decline of the great powers of the Fertile Crescent between the thirteenth and twelfth centuries B.C. Forcing their way into Asia Minor, they overthrew the Hittite empire, challenged for a while the might of Egypt and ultimately gained a foothold along the fertile Mediterranean coastland of southern Canaan. These enigmatic invaders, whose language and culture are still largely unknown to us, nearly succeeded in conquering all of the land. A relentless seesaw struggle ensued between them and the Israelites, with the issue long oscillating in the balance. Ultimately the Philistines were decisively defeated, leaving behind them destroyed cities, forming mounds that need to be excavated. They bequeathed to the country they failed to conquer an indelible memory of their presence in the name Palestine. The exact location of some of the cities of their Palestinian pentapolis escapes us, because the writers of the Bible did not find it necessary to furnish exact details. Its editors deemed it sufficient to their purposes to sketch in the nature and severity of the struggle, in order to highlight the workings of the will of God in history.

It is important constantly to bear in mind, however, that the full value of Biblical archaeology or archaeological exploration can be achieved only when they are pursued for objective historical information. It may be repeated for emphasis that the significance and authority of the spiritual insights and instruction of the Bible cannot be affected in any way whatsoever through archaeological confirmation of its historical statements. There is indeed always the possibility that some day an archaeological find will contradict an apparently historical fact in the Bible. If that unlikely contingency were to occur, it would merely indicate the fallibility of human beings whose judgments were too prejudiced, or whose knowledge was too limited, or whose observations were too imperfect to enable them to record history with unimpeachable accuracy. It would have no bearing whatsoever on the nature and applicability of Biblical truths or the validity of the Ten Commandments and would detract in no wise from the Bible's idea of God or its moral teachings.

The Biblical account of the collapse of the walls of Jericho cannot as yet be corroborated by the results of John Garstang's or Kathleen Kenyon's excavations at Tell es-Sultan (ancient Jericho). Erosion of mud-brick walls at the top of the tell may have removed the evidence. The available archaeological data are insufficient to permit a positive or negative conclusion. I myself am convinced that further investigation will attest to the historicity of the ecstatically reported phenomenon of the walls tumbling down in the time of Joshua. It makes no real difference, however, whether the tale proves to be accurate or not, because of paramount importance is the fact that it reflects the Bible's religious philosophy of the role of God in history.

It is most definitely not the purpose of Biblical archaeological exploration to "prove" the correctness of the testimony and teachings of the Bible. Indeed, I regard those people as being essentially of little faith who seek through archaeological corroboration of historical source materials in the Bible to validate its God concept and the ethical and moral structure dependent upon it. Either one believes in God and in the religion of the Bible or he disbelieves, but there is no possibility one way or another of empirical or rational proof. Faith in God does not come within the purview of the scientifically demonstrable.

Historical memory

Having thus affirmed that the correctness or infallibility of the theology of the Bible is not subject in any way whatsoever to archaeological "proof," we can nevertheless state equally emphatically that the results of Biblical archaeology have added enormously to a fuller understanding than otherwise possible of history in the Bible and of its language, literature, thought and cultural backgrounds. William F. Albright has been pre-eminent among those who have utilized archaeological materials to show that the early, preliterary, historical traditions of Israel preserved in the Bible are based upon amazingly correct historical facts and cannot be dismissed as later fabrications or "pious frauds." His discoveries and those of others have demonstrated that Biblical accounts dealing, for example, with the period of Abraham in the Middle Bronze Age I, dating between the twenty-first and nineteenth centuries B.C., reflect remarkably accurate memories of events which occurred at least a thousand years and more before they could possibly have been preserved in writing in the earliest records of the Bible.

It must be remembered that the Israelites of the Exodus and the generations of their descendants for whom the Bible was written in all probability knew nothing about the locations of most of the ancient sites that sprang up during the Age of Abraham and were cut down with catastrophic suddenness at the end of it. Yet somehow or other, for many centuries, the story of the past of the early Hebrews was transmitted by word of mouth in amazing detail, until finally the Biblical writers selected certain episodes of the oral history and immortalized them in writing in the pages of their religious testament.

The phenomenon of historical memory, harking back to preliterary periods, is not unique to the Bible. It is evidenced in the *Icelandic Tales* and in the *Rig Veda,* and is reflected most dramatically in the Homeric Epics and particularly in the *Iliad.* Heinrich Schliemann was the first to insist that the accounts in which Agamemmon of Mycenae, Menelaus and Helen of Sparta, Priam and Paris of Troy and Nestor of Pylos figured so prominently dealt with real people, events, places and objects and not merely with fanciful legends and mythological tales. He proved his point through archaeological undertakings, pushing back Greek history hundreds of years earlier than it was thought to have commenced.

Following in Schliemann's footsteps, Carl Blegen opened up the palace of Nestor at Pylos. There he discovered large numbers of clay tablets inscribed with the "Linear B" script, like those Evans had previously found at Knossos in Crete. The key to their unlocking has been furnished by the late brilliant young English scholar, Michael Ventris. When the tablets are completely deciphered, they may well accomplish for the understanding of the early Greek world what comparable Mesopotamian, Syrian, Palestinian and Egyptian discoveries have contributed to the deepening understanding of the early history of much of the Fertile Crescent and to the illumination of the backgrounds of the Bible.

"To seek and search out" (Ecclesiastes 1:13)
"The fountain of living waters" (Jeremiah 2:13)

While the archaeological explorer in Bible lands should first of all concern himself with historical information in the Bible, the second thing to do is to search for water. He who would rediscover the sites of ancient villages and towns and fortresses must first find out where springs or wells or perennial streams exist or once existed, and where cisterns and reservoirs were built. It is a truism, but one important to remember for the investigator of antiquity, that the location of an early settlement is almost always determined by the presence of an adequate water supply. Sometimes, particularly after the art of constructing watertight cisterns was developed, industrial or strategic reasons could be the decisive factors in site selection.

Water, in the imagery of the Bible, is pre-eminent as the symbol of man's greatest desires and needs, of ultimate power and of goodness. There are "three things that are never satisfied," according to Proverbs 30:15–16, "Sheol, the barren womb, and the earth ever thirsty for water." The reproach of the wicked in Job is that "You have given no water to the weary to drink" (Job 22:7). To be like "the water-courses in the Negev" (Psalm 126:4–6), transformed by spring freshets into rivers in the desert, expresses the hope of return from captivity. The Psalmist praises God with the words "Thou visitest the earth and waterest it" (Psalm 65:9). And in the language of the Bible, God equates the source of the blessing of water with His own Being: "They have forsaken Me, the fountain of living water" (Jeremiah

2:13). The irrigated field, the gushing spring, the perennial flow represented the height of blessing in the Bible: "You shall be like a watered garden, like a spring of water, whose waters fail not" (Isaiah 58:11).

"He hewed out many cisterns" (II Chronicles 26:10)

Perennial streams and springs and wells did not suffice as the population grew and the number of permanent settlements increased in the Holy Land. It became ever more necessary to hew out cisterns in impermeable rock or clay or make them watertight with several coats of plaster, and to terrace hillsides and dry stream-beds to catch the wayward rainwater and compel it to flow into cisterns or to percolate into the soil rather than permit it with unbraked force to wash the good earth away. Remaining for many months in suspension, the water stored thus in the sponge of the earth would suffice to nourish early-planted crops till they matured late in the dry season. In the Nabataean–Roman to Byzantine periods, between the second century B.C. and seventh century A.D., the art and science of soil and water conservation were advanced to an amazing degree. Whole ranges of hills were boldly employed as catchment basins. The pebbles on the upper parts of their slopes were swept aside into ordered piles, mistakenly called *teleilat el-anab* (grapevine hillocks), to expedite the runoff of rainwater along the paths thus cleared to the terraced wadi-beds below, as Professor Michael Evenari of the Hebrew University has proved.

It was particularly the invention of the cistern, however, seemingly not fully developed before the thirteenth century B.C., that helped inaugurate an economic revolution. Herds and flocks could be grazed wherever cistern water was made available for their nightly watering, and towns and fortresses built where no perennial streams or springs existed or wells could be dug. The name of the Judaean king Uzziah is hailed in the Bible because, among other accomplishments to his credit, "he built towers in the wilderness and he hewed out many cisterns" (II Chronicles 26:10). I have found many of them that may be attributed to Uzziah and his people and others to Solomon and his engineers before him. Circular, broad and deep for the most part, some of them are still nearly watertight to this day. Channels grooved diagonally in hillsides still serve to collect the runoff water from the hill-slopes and lead it into the cisterns.

Visit the forbidding lands of the northern part of the Nabataean kingdom commencing in northernmost Transjordan and marvel at the covered cisterns and the great reservoir of Umm el-Jemal. Examine with awe the tremendous, rock-hewn underground reservoir of Beit Ras, the site of ancient Capitolias in north central Transjordan, encircling part of a great hill, with apertures in the roof to receive the rainwater from the slopes above whenever the rains came. Gaze in wonderment at dams built by the Nabataeans and Romans and rebuilt by the Byzantines in the Wadi Kurnub, below the Nabataean-Byzantine city of Mampsis in the Negev, or at the one erected by the Romans across the Wadi Dhobai far out in the eastern desert of Transjordan. Find and list the places where energetic human beings throughout the centuries garnered every possible drop of rainwater, or made careful use of the flow of streams and springs, or dug into the earth to reach subterranean sources, and you will have a significant catalog of sites of human settlement and civilized activity from earliest historic and prehistoric times on.

"Highways and byways" (Judges 5:6)

There is a combination of other natural factors, in addition to the important one of water, that must be considered when searching for archaeological sites. It soon becomes apparent to the archaeological explorer that the geographic and topographic features of a country have conditioned in the past, as they must affect in all periods of the future, the story of man's going out and coming in, the choice of his places of settlement and routes of travel. Particularly in a relatively long and narrow country like greater Palestine, which includes Cisjordan and Transjordan, geographically oriented from north to south and hemmed in on the west by the Middle Sea (the Mediterranean) and on the east by the desert, the highways and the byways have always remained for all practical purposes unchangeably the same.

One recalls the pertinent passages in the famous Song of Deborah in Judges 5:6, 7: "In the days of Shamgar, the son of Anath, in the days of Jael, caravans ceased and travelers kept to the byways . . . until you arose, Deborah." Some highways and byways led through the Jordan Valley. The macadamized automobile road (Tariq es-Sultani) of today between

Damascus and Aqabah on the northeast shore of the Gulf of Aqabah is built in many places over or alongside the Roman road of Trajan, which followed the line of the preceding Biblical "King's Highway" (Numbers 21:22) and the still earlier track marked by settlements destroyed by the Kings of the East during the Age of Abraham (Genesis 14).

Along the ancient highways and byways, civilized settlements were established in prehistoric and historic times. In certain periods, as in the Age of Abraham between the twenty-first and nineteenth centuries B.C., more or less permanently inhabited centers sprang up anew, often on virgin soil. For many hundreds of years no sedentary occupation, marked by houses, pottery and tools, preceded or followed this Abrahamic era, at least in the Negev, the Wadi Arabah and most of Transjordan. Economic, political and military factors were almost always the reasons for the appearance, settlement, enrichment, decline, sudden destruction or gradual effacement of the sedentary civilized population. In the intervals of absence of civilization, rootless Bedouins roamed the land, leaving behind them no traces of their presence or passing. In other periods and regions, however, one village or town after another for many successive centuries would be erected on the ruins of its predecessor.

"A tell forever, an everlasting ruin" (Joshua 8:28)

The appearance of a tell

In much of the Holy Land during most of the earlier historic periods of settlement, it was natural for villages or towns of some size to provide their own protection and to function as if they were semi-independent city-states. The general rule, therefore, was for each community to select as a dwelling site an economically viable place, situated not only by an adequate water supply on or near some highway or crossroads, but preferably on a knoll or hill that could easily be fortified and whose very position would lighten the task of defense.

Approaches to a town that led up a fairly steep hillside could of course more easily be defended against an attacking force than paths across a plain. In addition, once the crown of the hill was covered with houses, a strong fortification wall surrounding it would enhance the natural strength of the elevation. Sometimes the security of a town would be further heightened by driving a shaft through its center until it pierced a water table or gave access to a spring far below, thus providing the inhabitants with assurance of water even if their walled fortress town were besieged. Such shafts of considerable depth, in vertical or horizontal form or both, have been found in Shobek and Qir-haresheth (Kerak) in Moab, in Lachish, Jerusalem, Gibeon, Gezer and Hazor in Judah and Israel. A somewhat similar underground approach to water existed at Zarethan (Tell es-Saidiyeh) in the Jordan Valley, as we shall later see. Extremely deep wells, sunk down 200 or more feet till they reached the water table, were not uncommon in Nabataean, Roman and Byzantine cities in the Negev. This fashion of providing safe access to water seems to have been in the mind of Isaiah, who proclaimed that he who seeks righteousness and shuns evil "shall dwell on high; his place of defence will be a rocky fortress; he shall not lack for bread and his water supply will be assured" (Isaiah 33:16).

In the course of time, the first walled settlement built on a particular rise would fall into ruin or be destroyed as a result of epidemic diseases, accidental conflagrations, earthquakes, economic desuetude or enemy attacks. The occasional ferocity of warfare resulting in the complete leveling of a town has been described in the Bible in these words: "And he took the city and slaughtered its inhabitants; and he razed the city and sowed it with salt" (Judges 9:45). The ruins of the settlement would soon be covered over with debris. Seeds of various plants would be wafted to the site or dropped by birds in passage, and soon it would become unrecognizable as having once been a place of habitation with houses and alleys and a surrounding fortification wall.

After the first village or town on a particular site had been abandoned or destroyed and had fallen into ruins and been covered over with windblown dirt, a second group of people—a year or ten or twenty-five or more years later—would decide to build a new walled city, and would perforce build it on top of the ruins of the first one. The same conditions that determined the location of the first walled settlement determined the location of the second. The newcomers had the limited choice either of digging up and removing the debris of the first settlement or of leveling it off and building a completely new walled town on top. The latter procedure was the one almost always adopted.

The practice of building one village upon the ruins of its predecessor led in the course of time to the formation of an artificial city-hill within which might be concealed the ruins of five or ten or more settlements built one on top of the other. Such a man-made mausoleum of destroyed cities, ultimately abandoned and concealing within itself the skeletal remains of many periods of building and fortification, is known as a tell in the Bible and in Hebrew and Arabic. Such a tell may be likened to a skyscraper, each city in it being comparable to a separate floor. In Biblical times, such high-rising museums of the past were already scattered over the landscape (Jeremiah 30:18; Joshua 11:13). There is mention in the Bible of a place becoming "a *tell* forever, an everlasting ruin" (Joshua 8:28).

It is fairly easy to recognize a tell. Located almost always on some kind of rise, commanding a view of the countryside round about, benefiting from the presence of water, nearby travel routes and some means of subsistence, a tell can usually be seen from afar. In appearance, it is more or less flat on top, with sides sloping rather abruptly downward and frequently with a mass of debris at its base. Such a tell is the tremendous Tell Abil, to be identified with the Biblical Abel-beth-maachah, overlooking the Huleh region in the northern Jordan Valley. The long, low, tree- and bush-covered Tell el-Qadi (the tell of the Judge), identified with the site of Biblical Dan, located at one of the sources of the Jordan, is less easily recognizable to the uninitiated. The comparatively small tell of ancient el-Hammeh, below Gadara, in the center of a small valley on the north side of the Yarmuk, can be distinguished even by the nonspecialist from the natural hills round about. The large, completely cultivated, partly artificial city-hill of Tell Maqlub, on the north side of the Wadi Yabis in North Gilead in Transjordan, is probably to be identified with the Biblical site of Abel-meholah. It possesses all the characteristics of a tell, from physical appearance to potsherds of various periods strewn on its surfaces.

"Potsherds of the earth" (Isaiah 45:9)

Even in Biblical times, fragments of pottery strewn on the dump heaps of every ancient site and representing the normal breakage of household earthenware, as well as part of the destructiveness of war, were familiar to the people of Israel and Judah and were referred to in picturesque similes (Isaiah 45:9).

The invention of pottery in the Neolithic period in the fifth millennium B.C. was one of mankind's greatest discoveries. It enabled a giant leap forward in the progress of civilization—a leap unequaled in many tens of thousands of years of previous development. Now food could be cooked and kept, stores of supplies set aside for comparatively prolonged periods of time, water carried for considerable distances, and surcease provided from daily efforts to procure food, thus releasing energies for new creative endeavors. Each era, from the pottery Neolithic period on, evolved its own styles, decorations and forms of pottery. Through empirical experience it is possible to recognize the variations from one age to another and thus to establish the date of a period of occupation from pottery discoveries alone and even from surface finds of pottery fragments. As a result both of commerce and conflict, foreign ceramic wares that influenced native products were often imported, adding firm and exact criteria, in addition to scarabs or coins, for dating purposes.

Pottery, once made either by hand or turned on a wheel, has thus outlasted tide and time. A pottery vessel can be shattered into hundreds of fragments but the sherds will not disintegrate because of age or attrition from exposure to the elements. Stone crumbles, copper and iron are consumed by corrosion; glass too is subject to decomposition and is known to change color and flake away under certain conditions. Wood, leather, papyrus, cloth and related materials vanish into thin air unless sealed off from moisture of any kind. Pottery, however, endures as an objective witness to the creative handiwork of human beings in a whole series of distinguishable periods. When baked earthenware became broken in the course of daily use or smashed because of man-made or natural catastrophes, the fragments were cast aside, littering the floors of rooms, the surfaces of streets and the sides of tells.

Flint tools of prepottery and pottery periods can be similarly employed for dating purposes, their ages established by comparable empirical methods and in part through geologic data.

Fashions of location

The archaeological explorer in Biblical lands necessarily becomes acquainted with the moods and manners of their particular periods of settlement. In the Middle Bronze I Age of Abraham, settlements were preferably located on broad hilltops and on long slopes open to the breezes, close

to cultivable fields and near some source of water. In the Iron Age period of
the kings of Israel and Judah most of the sites, with the exception of "open
villages," consisted of hilltop fortresses. Each guarded a source of water,
overlooked avenues of approach and cultivable fields or other sources of
livelihood, afforded refuge and protection in times of attack, and was in a
position through signals of smoke by day and fire by night to communicate
with at least two related sites on either side and consequently with a whole
chain of command in many directions. We have found it possible thus on
occasion in the Negev to venture the suggestion that a Judaean kingdom
fortress might well have been established on top of a distant hill visible from
the lookout point of a known fortress and then have the supposition confirmed by actual examination.

Later on, beginning with the Hellenistic–Nabataean–Roman era,
other criteria determined the location centers of habitation. The military
one diminished considerably in importance because of the widespread
peace the Pax Romana brought with it as a result of Roman military might
or the mere threat of its exercise. Radically changed building techniques
and much heavier types of foundations and structures introduced in this
period required a different kind of site than had usually been selected in
previous periods. The tendency was to move the monumental buildings
popular in the new age to level places out in the open, frequently on virgin
soil and sometimes quite a distance removed from the original hilltop fortresses. This did not always occur, to be sure, because often a Nabataean- or
Roman-period structure was superimposed upon a preceding Judaean or
Edomite or Moabite or even earlier one, but it happened often enough to
become a common phenomenon.

With and without names

Sometimes an ancient site, tell or not, has carried essentially the same name
down through history. Thus Tell Arad in the northern Negev is undoubtedly the last in a long succession in the Arad district of the Bible, even as
the name of Beersheba has remained unchanged for thousands of years.
Examples of this kind could be multiplied. There come to mind place
names in the Jordan Valley like Eriha (Jericho), Beisan (Beth–shan),
Damieh (Adamah), Tell Abil (Abel–beth–maachah) which faithfully reflect

the ancient originals. It behooves the archeological explorer, therefore, to pay attention to modern designations in his search for ancient sites. Caution is called for, of course, because frequently, as previously noted, an ancient Biblical name will have moved in the Hellenistic–Roman period some distance away from its original home to a new site, first established after the original Biblical one had been abandoned or destroyed.

Over half the sites discovered in the Jordan Valley can be dated to the Iron I period beginning in the twelfth century B.C. The Biblical editors were probably familiar with the locations of most of these latter sites, as well as with their histories and traditions, yet they mentioned only nine. Why did they fail to describe or even list all of them in their records? Indeed, the very paucity of names of Biblical sites in the Jordan Valley helped to give currency to the notion that it was largely abandoned in Biblical times. It has been thought that the region was used then mainly for grazing, and was visited only during the planting and harvesting seasons in the early spring and late summer.

The explanation is not far to seek. For the Bible to have mentioned every one of the thirty-five or more Israelite places dating between the twelfth and sixth centuries B.C. which have now been discovered on the east side of the Jordan Valley alone would have been contrary to the method and purpose of its editors. They were interested neither in furnishing a list of all towns in any given district nor in writing a historical geography of the Holy Land or a list of place names of Palestine. For them all history was included under religion. Places and people and incidents were discussed only insofar as they helped make clear the overriding theological purposes of the Bible.

It should come as no surprise, therefore, that of all the Biblical sites which from archaeological evidence we know existed in the rich lands of the north half of the east side of the Jordan Valley, there are mentioned, for instance, going from north to south, only Jabesh-gilead, Zaphon, Zarethan, Succoth and Adamah.

Method of presentation

Ancient sites found as a result of surface exploration do not occur in any historical sequence but in a completely jumbled lack of relationship in time

I I / A river is born

The enigma of the Jordan

The Jordan is a weird stream of limitless sanctity to many millions of people. It twists and tears its way steeply downward in an almost incredibly sinuous manner from the sweet waters of the Sea of Galilee to the stinging wastes of the Sea of Salt (the Dead Sea). Squirming frantically, burrowing madly, seeking wildly to escape its fate, the Jordan's course from its crystal-clear beginnings to its dark and bitter end is a helpless race to a hopeless goal. Like Lot's wife, it looks backward only inevitably to perish in the deep abyss of the Bahr Lut, the Sea of Lot, as the Arabs call it.

In neither size, volume, length nor utility is the Jordan River pre-eminent or even notable among the rivers of the world. When I first saw it, I was taken aback. It did not begin to measure up in size to my mental image of the Jordan which looms so large in the Biblical narrative and plays such a legendary role in religious history. It appears insignificant compared to the Tigris and Euphrates in Mesopotamia, the Nile in Egypt and many others such as the Mississippi, the Amazon, the Danube, the Volga, the Indus and the Yangtze. Nevertheless, the Jordan equals or surpasses them all in physical variety, historical importance and spiritual significance.

Earthquake-born

Titanic upheavals and massive faulting or shattering of the surface of the earth going back to early geologic ages preceded and affected the present configuration of the Jordan Valley, the Dead Sea and the Wadi Arabah. They are contained in part of the great north–south rift that extends from Asia to Africa. Transverse faults at an oblique angle helped produce on the east side of the Jordan and of the Dead Sea the four great river valleys known today (moving from north to south) as the Yarmuk, the Wadi Zerqa (Biblical Jabbok), the Wadi Mojib (Biblical Arnon) and the Wadi Hesa (Biblical Zered).

The Jordan Valley assumed its present form before the Late (Upper) Pleistocene Age of the Upper Palaeolithic period came to an end about twelve to fifteen thousand years ago. At that time the single extensive body of water called the "Lisan" lake, which had stretched from the region of the Sea of Galilee to the Wadi Arabah, broke up into two completely separate smaller units. One formed the Sea of Galilee and the other the Dead Sea.

Between these two lakes the Jordan River came into being. It proceeded to cut its way down through the disarranged and intermingled levels of the formerly water-covered fault, by the sides of which the Ubeidiyan anthropoids of the Lower Palaeolithic Age (before ca. 70,000 B.C.) had once lived and hunted, making use of Pebble Culture tools and weapons. Several levels of terraces were formed in the Jordan Valley as a result of various periods of shrinking of the "Lisan" lake. The lowest river bed, the Zor, through which the Jordan cleaves its path, lies in the "Lisan" marls that had been deposited at the bottom of the "Lisan" lake. This name stems from the fact that the clay and gypsum sediments at the bottom of this landlocked body of water are similar to those of the peninsula called the Lisan (tongue) extending into the Dead Sea from its east shore.

It was at Tell Ubeidiya in the Wadi el-Amud on the west bank of the Jordan, less than two miles south of the Sea of Galilee, that Moshe Stekelis excavated, among other fauna, remains of an incisor tooth and two highly primitive skull fragments of a human being, termed Sinanthropus. These exciting skull remains, the earliest thus far known in the Near East, are four times as thick as the skull of a modern man.

The Pebble Culture implements used by the Ubeidiyan man are so named because they were formed from crude large pebbles found in clay and gravel beds of the Early Pleistocene Age of the Lower Palaeolithic period in the Jordan Valley. The pebbles were given sharp cutting edges by removing flakes in two opposite directions at one end. Also found were roughly trimmed semispherical balls, choppers, and trihedral pointed tools that seem to be precursors of handaxes.

To judge from the animal bones found at Tell Ubeidiya, the early Nimrods there hunted elephants, hippopotami, rhinoceroses, zebras and bears among a total of more than fifty different specimens. Utilizing flint instruments, they split the bones, as can be seen from cutting marks on them, to extract the marrow. Another Pebble Culture site has been located at Khirbet Maskana, a short distance to the north-northwest of Tell Ubeidiya, on a hill overlooking the Jordan Valley from the west and relatively close to Tiberias.

Thus it is seen that the Jordan Valley and river have evolved out of the convulsions and changes of an immense span of time. A close examination of the length of the entire Jordan Rift, traveling southward from the base of Mount Hermon to the north shore of the Gulf of Aqabah, the eastern arm of the Red Sea, reveals all kinds of rock formations spanning distant geologic ages. To be seen are black fields or outcroppings of basalt, fantastically cut slopes of chalky marl, sands glittering with fool's gold, treacherously soft salty wastes, reddish-brown stretches of hematite hills, dun-colored ranges streaked with coppery green, shattered sheets of glinting flint.

The competent observer would understand that the floor of the great rift is an unsteady one, subject to mighty fissuring pressures and resting in many places on burning or cooling foundations. Health-seekers still frequent the famous hot springs of Tiberias on the Sea of Galilee and of el-Hammeh near the outlet of the Yarmuk River into the Jordan. Many people also bathe in the equally famous hot springs of Callirhoe, located close to where the Wadi Zerqa Main empties into the northeast end of the Dead Sea.

Quiescent volcanoes and filled-in craters can be seen along the length of the Jordan fault. One of the northernmost craters contains the pond of Birket er-Ram (Lake Phiala), to the east of the Banias source of the Jordan. Earthquakes resulting from restless shifting of the earth have destroyed cities in the Jordan Valley as large as Jericho, have caused landslides that dammed up the Jordan (Joshua 3:16, 17) and have shaken the threshold of the Temple in Jerusalem (Isaiah 6:4; cf. Numbers 16:30–31; Psalms 18:7; 29:8; Amos 1:1; Zechariah 14:5). The Temple area in Jerusalem is on a line of structural weakness in the rock foundations of the earth, and the Mosque el-Aqsa built over it has, as a result, suffered frequently from earthquakes, as has the Church of the Holy Sepulchre.

One great convulsion created the immense sinkhole of the Dead Sea. The shrinking waters of the "Lisan" lake were imprisoned in the almost incredibly deep chasm, the top of which is 1286 feet below sea level and the bottom of which is once again as deep. In it the waters of the Jordan find their grave. There, compounded with salts and sulphur and other chemicals drawn from the bowels of the earth, they are intermingled with the witches' brew now known as the Dead Sea.

Josephus reported some two millennia ago that the Dead Sea was called the Asphalt Lake. The bitumen or asphalt periodically spewed up from its depths was much prized in ancient times. I have come across it in my explorations. The Nabataeans, the Judeaeans before them and still earlier the people of the Abrahamic period exported it to Egypt, where it was used for embalming. Archaeological finds by Yohanan Aharoni and Ruth Amiran at Tell Arad, east of Beersheba in the northernmost Negev, revealed imported jars of the type found in Abydos in Egypt, together with chunks of bitumen (pitch, asphalt) from the Dead Sea, indicating the two-way trade between Arad and Egypt at the time of the First Dynasty, nearly a millennium before the time of Abraham.

*P*alaeoanthropus Palestinensis

In prehistoric times a life of tropical abundance flourished in the Jordan Valley. Numerous animals, most of them now extinct, roamed about there. Skeletal remains of various species of fauna and tusks of elephants have been found in places extending from the Mediterranean coastal plain to a garden on the highest point of Bethlehem located in the Judaean hills, a few miles south-southwest of Jerusalem, to sites immediately above or directly on the western bank of the Jordan. One of the sites is close to Jisr Banat Yaaqub, the "Bridge of the Daughters of Jacob," which crosses the

Jordan north of the Sea of Galilee. Indeed, among the remains dug up from the ancient bed of the Jordan was an elephant's tusk 6 feet long.

The elephant hunters of the Jordan Valley, who lived long after their most primitive Ubeidiyan predecessors, were related to the prehistoric Galilee man whose Neanderthaloid skull was discovered in the cave of Mugharet ez-Zuttiyeh in the Wadi el-Amud in the hills overlooking the Sea of Galilee. It is dated to the period extending from about 50,000 to about 70,000 B.C. Not far removed from the Galilee Man in time and space are the human remains unearthed in the cave of Jebel Qafze near Nazareth.

Best preserved of all were the skeletons of Palestine Man (Palaeoanthropus Palestinensis) excavated by Dorothy Garrod and T. D. McCown in caves near Mount Carmel overlooking the Mediterranean. Encased and wonderfully preserved in a hard limestone breccia formed by limestone sediment of water dripping from the roofs of the caves around them, they may be dated to the end of the first part of the Middle Palaeolithic period, from about 50,000 to about 40,000 years ago. The skeletons show a range from a Neanderthal-type woman to a man with some strikingly modern characteristics, and all had undergone great development since the time of their very-much-earlier Ubeidiyan predecessors.

The men and women of the Homo Palestinensis type of the Mount Carmel caves of Tabun represented a mixture of races resulting from Palestine's position as an intercontinental bridge, as Albright and others have pointed out. Their skeletons indicate a mixture of races ranging from Palaeoanthropic Man (Homo Neanderthalis) to Neanthropic Man (Homo Sapiens). Small bands found shelter in natural caves, in which or near which they buried their dead in positions and under circumstances indicating some kind of primitive religious orientation. They hunted big game, roasted some of their meat, fashioned excellent flint tools and weapons and made ornaments to decorate their bodies. They could walk and probably talk after a fashion and seem not to have been too dissimilar in appearance from some types of modern man.

The driving prepossession of primitive man with hunting and food-gathering began to change at the end of the Upper Palaeolithic period, 12,000 to 15,000 years ago, when traceable beginnings of tilling the soil and raising food commenced. This development took place with increasing intensity during the Mesolithic–Natufian (named for a site in the Wadi en-Natuf, near Mount Carmel) or Middle Stone Age, which lasted until the beginning of the Neolithic period about 8000 B.C. At that time, at least in the Fertile Crescent, agriculture began intensively to revolutionize the life of the human species.

The arts of agriculture, animal husbandry, architecture, metallurgy, pottery-making and weaving were unknown to Homo Palestinensis. He was blessed with few possessions. By the time of his Natufian descendants or successors, however, the Modern Era had emerged. Its unfolding in the subsequent Neolithic period, commencing about ten millennia ago, was rapid and radical. People began in ever-increasing measure to plant and reap crops, raise animals, build houses, weave baskets, fashion ornaments, engage in trade and find further expression in sculpture and painting, although the latter had first appeared much earlier in human history. Therewith ended the idyllic simplicity of the early ages. Man and woman left the Garden of Eden. With these various activities began the turbulent history of civilization in the Jordan Valley and the rest of Palestine. Its account has been volcanic ever since.

The change in the kind of men and women who peopled early Palestine may be correlated with important changes in climate. These occurred across a long period extending approximately from about half a million years ago when a damp and tropical climate prevailed, during which rhinoceroses, hippopotami and elephants were plentiful, to a dry, warm climate at the beginning of the Natufian period, when gazelles and deer became abundant. From that day to this, there have been no major, permanent climatic changes in Palestine or the Near East—or probably anywhere on the face of the earth, although cyclical and extremely limited variations of weather, and particularly of moisture, may have occurred.

The Valley of the Lebanon

The fairest part of the great geologic fault to which the Jordan Valley belongs is the Valley of the Lebanon. That is the literal translation of Biqath ha-Lebanon, as it is called in the Bible (Joshua 11:17). Hemmed in by the cypress-and-cedar-adorned Lebanon Mountains on the west side and by the anti-Lebanon range on the east, the valley was once called "Hollow Syria" (Coele-Syria), a name loosely applied at times to all of southern Syria with the exception of Phoenicia. At the time of the Seleucids, it included the territory around Damascus (I Maccabees 10:69; II Maccabees 3:5, 8). The fertile fields and strong streams of the extensive Lebanon Valley have helped fill it with cities and settlements from earliest antiquity. Their glittering crown was the fabulous city and sanctuary of Baalbek.

The founding fathers of Baalbek worshiped many pagan deities there, among the chief of whom was the male god of fertility. Baal was his name. The Greeks, much later, had another word for it. They, or rather the Hellenized Syrians, identified him with the Greek sun god, Helios. In his honor the name of Baalbek was changed to Heliopolis, only to revert to its original designation, retained to this day, after the sun of Greek culture had set. This occurred in the seventh century A.D. with the advent of Islam, at the end of the Byzantine period in the Near East, which had been marked by the brilliant union of cultural Hellenism and burgeoning Christianity.

The Romans erected resplendent temples at Baalbek to some of their many gods. Byzantine Christians transformed these shrines into churches and basilicas, which Moslems changed into citadels and mosques. Mongols came then to destroy and massacre, and meanwhile earthquakes had their disastrous innings too. Even in their ruins, the remains of the original structures of Baalbek stand in imposing majesty. Six of the mighty columns of the Temple of Jupiter, each 62 feet high and 7½ feet in diameter, still hold themselves proudly erect. Their glorious Corinthian capitals command a distant view over the watered greenness of the Valley of the Lebanon.

North of Baalbek, on the far side of the small lake of Homs, the Orontes River (Nahr el-Asi) commences its northward course, to turn westward ultimately and flow through the ancient city of Antioch at a point about twenty miles from its outlet into the Mediterranean. The evangelical efforts of early Christianity proved most fruitful at Antioch. There "Saul who is called Paul" and Barnabas taught in the church to which they returned at journey's end (Acts 11:19–26; 13:1–3, 14; 14:26). It was at Antioch by the Orontes that the converts to the new faith, preached with such Jewish passion by Paul and Barnabas, were called "Christians" (Acts 11:26). Well to the south of the Lake of Homs[1] and

[1] The Lake of Homs marks approximately the idealized northernmost limit of the Solomonic kingdom, described in the Bible as reaching to the "entrance of Hamath" (Judges 3:3; I Kings 8:65; Amos 6:14).

several miles to the south of Baalbek the Leontes River (Nahr Litani) comes into being. Its stream flows south-southeastward to hug the base of the Lebanon Mountains, until it cuts a deep canyon through them and cascades westward to reach and enrich part of the Phoenician coast with its waters before emptying into the Mediterranean at a point north of Tyre. High in the hills, commanding the sharp bend in the river, the Crusaders built the magnificent fortress of Belfort (Qalat esh-Shaqif) whose massive shell bears eloquent testimony to the herculean thrust and evanescent success of their monumental undertakings.

*T*he sources of the river

The meaning of the name

South of Baalbek the union of four streams, born of springs originating from the snows of Mount Hermon, creates the river that became known as the Jordan. The name superficially seems to mean "the Descender" or "the River-that-goes-down." The fact that a river flows downward is characteristic of all rivers, however. Some of them, like the Jordan, descend more precipitately than others. The root of the word "Jordan" may more correctly be related to the Arabic root "wrd," as several scholars have suggested, conveying the idea of people and flocks making their way to a source of water. That would conform to what the Jordan is sometimes called by Arabs, namely, *esh-Sharia*, meaning "The Drinking Place." Washed white with snow at its beginnings, the Jordan soon acquires a muddy coloring as it pursues its frenzied journey. The climactic end occurs when it flings itself and its heavy burden of silt far into the murky waters of the Dead Sea.

Mount Hermon

Towering high above the sources of the river is Mount Hermon, whose hoary head lends it grave and beautiful distinction. The Jebel esh-Sheikh, "the Mountain Chieftain," to give it its Arabic name, dominates most of the length of the geologic fault of the Jordan. In the *Targumim*, the Aramaic translations of the Bible, the majestic rockpile of Mount Hermon is known as the Tur Talga, "the Mountain of Snow." Walking in the Jordan Valley on a torrid summer day at a point not far from Jericho, I have glimpsed from afar its white mantle. I have, furthermore, often seen its silvery mane mirrored in the frequently calm waters of the Sea of Galilee, whose existence depends in the final analysis on the bounty of the mountain's melting snows. And when, sometimes, the summer's sun melts most of the snow away, dulling the patriarchal appearance of the commanding pinnacle, the sinews of its massive bulk become all the more apparent.

The Hermon range extends from northeast to southwest for a distance of nearly twenty miles. Its principal peak, resembling an immense truncated cone, is divided into three parts. The highest reaches up 9232 feet above sea level, with the other two only a little lower. Little wonder then that this stalwart sentinel was anciently dedicated to divinity and considered the abode of gods. The temple of the chief of them, called Baal-hermon (Judges 3:3), graced its summit, and it was natural for shrines to be strewn around its base.

"As far as Mount Hermon" was a Biblical phrase full of meaning to multitudes whose lives were influenced by its fountains, to travelers whose gaze was lifted toward the familiar landmark and to armies for which it was variously a bulwark and barrier. Many nations knew it, some by other names. The Bible tells us that Mount Hermon was called Sirion by the Sidonians, while the Amorites called it Senir (Deuteronomy 3:9). The grandeur of its repose brought quiet to the disturbed, as witnessed by the prayer of the Psalmist: "My soul is cast down within me, therefore I remember thee from the land of Jordan and [the hills of Mount] Hermon . . ." (Psalms 42:6).

Branches of the beginning

NAHR BANIAS

The easternmost of the streams rising at the base of Mount Hermon is the Nahr (River) Banias. It is only about five and a half miles long, but the manner of its origin has impelled human beings from early times to reflect on the mystery of creation. To reach the headwaters of the Banias, the visitor crosses a small deep gorge, through which the stream rushes shortly after coming into being. Not far above it is a flat, boulder-strewn meadow, garlanded with brush, fern, oleander bushes, grass and a rainbow variety of wild flowers in season, which try but fail to conceal numerous little rivulets of water darting between them. Gurgling and frolicking and growing rapidly in size, they join together and split apart in an endless game of hide-and-seek before finally uniting into a single stream. To anyone acquainted with the arid Near East, where water is more prized than gold and precious jewels, the sight of all this wealth gladdens the heart.

The amazement and elation of the onlooker grow apace as one advances to the very birthplace of this blessing. A great, precipitous, iron-reddened, limestone cliff looms up. In it is a large cave, earthquake battered. From its base there bursts forth a rushing, foaming little stream that seems to shout as it emerges: "Get out of my way, for here I come." Like a lively child it plunges into play, moving so rapidly that it seems to be running in different directions at the same time and singing loud and clear. The sweet melody can be heard from afar. The pilgrim's spontaneous reaction to this happy phenomenon of newborn life is to be lost in awe and wonder. It is impossible not to be aware of the fact that this stream helps form the fabled Jordan, whose flow is one of unique significance in the course of history.

Throughout the ages, altars and sanctuaries were constructed at this spot and uninhibited festivities celebrated in nearby groves. Was this perhaps the seat of "Baal-gad in the Valley of the Lebanon" (Joshua 12:7)? And what was more natural for the Greeks or those suffused with Greek culture to do when they sought to glorify this womb of waters than to dedicate the cave whence they emerged to one of their gods—the vigorous and lustful Pan, accompanied by his playmates, the nymphs! No more appropriate place could be imagined where he could skip and leap with heathenish abandon than this fecund spot. Reference to Pan and the nymphs appears in the first line of a Greek inscription on the face of the rock above the entrance to the cave, reading in the equivalent of Latin characters PANI TE KAI NYMPHAIS. It was entirely in keeping therefore for the name of Paneion to be applied to this particular place and that of Panaeas to the nearby town and to the district in which it was located.

Name changes Paneas underwent several name changes, but none of them found lasting acceptance among the native inhabitants. When the rise of

Islam in the seventh century A.D. marked the end of the Byzantine period and the withering away of Hellenistic culture in the ancient Near East, the name Paneas, which apparently had never been forgotten, came to the fore again and has remained in use. The Arabs know it as Baneas, because the letter *p* frequently becomes a *b* in their speech and sometimes an *f*, as in modern Feinan for Biblical Punon.

The first change of name was instituted by Herod Philip (4 B.C.–A.D. 34), tetrarch of the mainly mountainous districts, including Paneas, to the north and east of the Sea of Galilee. This territory had been assigned him in accordance with the last will of his father, Herod the Great (37–4 B.C.). The rest of his father's domain was partitioned between his other two surviving half-brothers, Herod Antipas and Archelaus (the eldest). The mother of Antipas and Archelaus was the Samaritan Malthace; Herod Philip's mother was the Graeco-Egyptian Cleopatra of Jerusalem. Herod Antipas (4 B.C.–A.D. 39) was made tetrarch of Galilee and Peraea (meaning "the Beyond" in Greek and extending along most of the east side of the Jordan Valley and the east side of the north half of the Dead Sea). Archelaus (4 B.C.–A.D. 6), with the title of ethnarch, was put in charge of Samaria, Judaea and Idumaea. When he was banished by Augustus to Gaul, even as Herod Antipas later was to be exiled by Caligula, his territory was placed for many years under the direct rule of a series of Roman procurators. The best-remembered of these procurators is Pontius Pilate (A.D. 26–36), who decreed the crucifixion of Jesus.

Neither individually nor collectively did the three who inherited separate regions of their father's domain prove his equal, let alone his better. The brutal Herod the Great had not gotten around to having them murdered, as he had had his other sons, before he died in 4 B.C. Apparently convinced that no one of them could rule singly in his stead, he divided his realm, apparently with Roman approval, into three parts, placing each of his surviving sons in authority over a district.

It seems that whenever a really strong and gifted leader like Herod the Great appeared upon the Palestinian scene—one who could ride herd for better or worse on his family, placate or dominate the often diametrically opposed factions among his people and successfully gain or court the favor of the dominant world power—he was able to unite the entire country of ancient Israel and Judah under his sole command. Solomon had set the classic example. It was repeated under the Hasmonean Alexander

Jannaeus (103–76 B.C.), occurred again under Herod the Great and for a brief interval under his grandson Herod Agrippa I (A.D. 41–44). In each instance it was as if several separate gravitational fields were pulled together by the magnet of a powerful personality, only to fall apart again upon his death.

With the death of Herod Agrippa I, this process came to an end among the Judaeans, even as did the union, represented in his person, of their two most powerful and mutually antagonistic families, the Hasmoneans and the Herodians. Agrippa's father Aristobulus was one of the sons executed by Herod the Great in his maniacal fears of his later years. His grandmother Mariamne, the mother of Aristobulus, a Hasmonean princess whom Herod the Great had taken to wife to cement the relations between the two families, had likewise been put to death by her wildly neurotic husband.

It is interesting to note that the beginning and end of Herodian rule of any kind in Palestine is connected with the site that first appears in our story under the name Paneas. Herod the Great received the entire district of Paneas as a present from Augustus Caesar (27 B.C.–A.D. 14), which was the title Octavian assumed when be became the sole head of the Roman empire. To show his appreciation, Herod built in honor of his patron a temple of white marble on a hilltop there. At the bottom of the hill was the cave whence issued the waters forming one of the sources of the Jordan.

After the death of Herod the Great, Paneas became part of the inheritance of his son Herod Philip, who rebuilt the town and established his capital there. In accordance with a time-tested precept followed by practically all the members of his family whenever possible, he changed the name of Paneas to that of Caesarea,[2] to curry favor with the ruler of the Roman Empire. (Actually, he was following the example previously set by his father. When Herod the Great built a magnificent seaport over the site of Strato's tower on the Mediterranean coast of Palestine, he gave it the name Caesarea in honor of the same Augustus.) To distinguish between the two places, Herod Philip's Caesarea became known as Caesarea Philippi,[3] while the earlier one figured in history as Caesarea Maritima or Caesarea-on-the-Sea. It was at Caesarea Maritima that Pontius Pilate established his residence when he became procurator of Judaea. Paul was to become well acquainted with it.

[2] Josephus, *Antiquities*, XVIII, ii, 1.   [3] Matthew 16:13; Mark 8:27.

HEROD AGRIPPA II   Less than a quarter of a century after the death in A.D. 34 of Herod Philip (the only one of the sons of Herod the Great to die in office), the name of Caesarea (Philippi), introduced by him in place of Paneas, underwent yet another temporary change. It was called Neronias, after the Roman emperor Nero (A.D. 54–68). This change occurred under Philip's grandnephew Herod Agrippa II (A.D. 50–100), son of Herod Agrippa I and a great-grandson of Herod the Great. Herod Agrippa II was also the brother of two beautiful women whose lives became intertwined with the history and character of his times. The most famous, or perhaps most tragic, of them was Berenice.

Berenice had already been wed and widowed when at the age of thirteen she was married to her uncle, Herod of Chalcis, brother of her father Herod Agrippa I, in A.D. 41. Widowed again in A.D. 48, Berenice entered into an incestuous relationship with her brother Herod Agrippa II. Born in A.D. 27, he was a year older than she. The liaison of the two, respectively twenty-one and twenty years of age when it commenced, afforded Juvenal occasion for some acid remarks.[4] After a while, Berenice married Ptolemon, king of Cilicia (where Tarsus, the home of Paul, was located),[5] but soon deserted him to return to her brother's couch. The Biblical rules of chastity meant as little to her as they had earlier to her older relative Herodias, who had a penchant for marrying her half-uncles without waiting for one to die before abandoning him and taking on the second.

It was while visiting Caesarea Maritima on the Mediterranean coast of Palestine with her brother and lover, Herod Agrippa II, that both of them had occasion to attend and take part in verbal exchanges in the equivalent of a court case being presided over by the Roman procurator Porcius Festus (A.D. 60–62). At issue was the demand made by Paul, arrested on the charge of disturbing the public peace, to be sent to Rome in accordance with his citizen-rights to argue his case before the imperial tribunal.[6] Berenice and Herod Agrippa II had come to Caesarea "to welcome Festus" (Acts 25:13), the successor of their brother-in-law, Antonius Felix, whose wife was their sister Drusilla (Acts 24:24).

Later, during the mature bloom of her beauty, Berenice became the mistress of Titus, the future Roman emperor. At the time, he was engaged

---

[4] Juvenal, *Satire*, VI: lines 155–157; Tacitus, *Hist.* ii, 2.   [5] Acts 9:11; 21:39; 22:3.
[6] Acts 25:13–26:32.

in crushing the Judaean rebellion against Rome, which lasted from A.D. 66 to 73. Accompanying Titus to Rome, Berenice dared to dream of sharing the throne there with him. However, when in A.D. 79 Titus became emperor, he dismissed her for reasons of state and compelled her to return to her own country. This famous love affair has been immortalized by Racine, who depicts Berenice as a fascinating woman of deepest sensitivity and most passionate nature.[7]

Berenice's brother, Herod Agrippa II, being only seventeen years old when his father, Herod Agrippa I, died in A.D. 44, was long considered by the Roman authorities too young to be entrusted with the stewardship of his father's kingdom. The territory governed by Herod Agrippa I had been expanded by a series of gains, as a result of the favor of the Roman emperor Claudius (A.D. 41–54). For a few years, between A.D. 41–44, the domain of Herod Agrippa I included all the area once governed by his grandfather Herod the Great and by Alexander Jannaeus and Solomon before him. This came about in several successive stages:

In A.D. 37, through the favor of Gaius Caesar Caligula (A.D. 37–41), Herod Agrippa I, the son of Aristobulus, whose father, Herod the Great, had had him executed, succeeded one of his uncles, Herod Philip, as tetrarch of Auranitis, Batanaea, Ituraea and Panaeas. Two years later the Roman emperor turned over to him also the tetrarchy of another uncle, Herod Antipas, whom he exiled to Gaul in A.D. 39.

Two years after the downfall of Herod Antipas, the ethnarchate of Samaria, Judaea and Idumaea, originally willed by Herod the Great to his eldest son, Archelaus, was added to the territory of the conscienceless Herod Agrippa I by the Roman emperor Claudius. When Archelaus was exiled to Gaul in A.D. 6 by Caesar Augustus, his ethnarchate was placed under the direct authority of Roman procurators, among whom was Pontius Pilate.

The rule of Roman procurators was briefly interrupted when the entire country was reunited for a few years (A.D. 41–44) under Herod Agrippa I. Thereafter and until the Judaean rebellion broke out in A.D. 66, Roman procurators again became the immediate governors of Samaria, Judaea and Idumaea, subject to a Roman legate who resided in Syria. It was, indeed, their harshness that brought on the suicidal revolt, resulting in unmitigated

---

[7] Racine, *Berenice*, translated by John Masefield in *Esther and Berenice*, pp. 109ff.

disaster, particularly for Judaea. Herod Agrippa II, the son of Herod Agrippa I, was to live through it all in incredible peace with his Roman masters, as if the slaughter of his brethren, the ravaging of Jerusalem and the three-year siege and fall of the last-ditch stronghold of Masada were taking place on another planet.

Had Herod Agrippa II been of age when his father died in A.D. 44, it is conceivable that the Romans might have permitted him to reign over the entire country. Not, however, until A.D. 50, when he was twenty-three, did the Roman emperor Claudius toss him a crumb of territory, together with a fancy title. He made him king of the city and district of Chalcis, located to the north and east of the Sea of Galilee and between the districts of Abilene and Ituraea.

Fortune smiled on Herod Agrippa II three years later, when he must have been considered mature enough to be given greater responsibility. Instead of his little kingdom of Chalcis, he received through Roman favor the much more important territory that his grand-uncle Herod Philip had inherited from Herod the Great. It included the town and district of Paneas. In addition, he received the tetrarchy of Abilene, near Damascus, which had formerly been governed by Lysanias (Luke 3:1).

The imperial favor accorded Herod Agrippa II was further enlarged when Nero succeeded Claudius as emperor of Rome. Nero not only confirmed the rule of Herod Agrippa II over these tetrarchies, but also added to them the rich province of Galilee. To show his gratitude, Herod Agrippa II resorted to a device often employed by members of his family before him—changing the name of Caesarea Philippi at the Banias headwaters of the Jordan to Neronias. The assumption is that Nero, his powerful but (according to possibly apocryphal legend) somewhat deranged benefactor, was much edified thereby. Among the Roman coins of the town may be seen one with the laureled head of Apollo on the obverse side, and on the reverse the figure of Poppaea, Nero's queen, portrayed as being inside a pillared temple. The demonstrativeness of Nero's affection for his queen evidenced on the coin is somewhat less than touching in view of the fact that in a fit of temper he first kicked her to death and then in an excess of remorse had her proclaimed a goddess.

Rome never had reason to rue the benefactions of Claudius and Nero to Herod Agrippa II. Throughout his reign of a half a century he remained utterly loyal, even when his compatriots were engaged in fierce and futile six-year rebellion in Judaea against Rome. Let it be said to the credit of Herod Agrippa II that he tried to dissuade his brethren from the rash and foredoomed uprising, although he kept completely aloof when they failed to heed him. Had he lived in a later period, he would in all probability have stood aside also in the Bar Kochba rebellion against Rome, which flamed fiercely for three years (A.D. 132–135) before it could be smothered.

On the whole, it may be said that the Roman Empire was well served by its Herodian vassals. In many ways, by education, upbringing and association, they were more Roman than Jewish. By and large, however, they did as well as they possibly could and sometimes performed brilliantly for their country, or various parts of it, in view of the prevailing configuration of international power politics. In spite of their driving ambitions, ruthless behavior and religious cynicism, they brought many benefits to their people through their political acumen and governing abilities.

The family motto of the Herodians might well have been that what was good for Rome was good for them and all of their country and people. This was certainly true of Herod Agrippa I, who most properly had himself designated on some of his coins as *philoromais*, "friend of the Romans." His son Herod Agrippa II was no less Rome-oriented, and remained so through thick and thin. As a result his territories in the northernmost part of the country were neither invaded nor despoiled, and he was permitted to exercise his authority over them until his death in A.D. 100. Only then were his tetrarchies incorporated into the Roman province of Syria, 127 years after Judaea had been made a Roman dependency by Pompey. Never again was Panaeas (Caesarea Philippi, Neronias), under any name whatsoever, to be the capital of an Herodian prince.

History has shown, however, that it made no difference at all to the inhabitants of the land whether the name of Paneas was changed to Caesarea Philippi or Neronias. Pan remained their patron god and Paneas a center of his worship. It continued to be known to them as such, whatever the vagaries and motivations of passing princes in periodically changing its name to flatter foreign emperors. The names and traditions of the country were perpetuated in the memories and speech of the people of the land, to whom it made precious little difference under whose rule they lived and into whose coffers the taxes wrung from them were siphoned. Neither the passage of time nor the periodic change of guard could divert them from what was immovably theirs—the watered land, the familiar gods and the use of the old place names whose significance and appeal could not be eradicated by governmental fiat.

"Get Thee Behind Me, Satan" (Matthew 16:23)   The scent of pagan sanctity hovered long over Paneas—even after Christianity became the official religion of the eastern Roman empire through the conversion of Constantine I and the establishment of Byzantium as his capital early in the fourth century A.D. Eusebius in his *Church History* mentions some of the heathenish practices still practiced then at Paneas:

At Caesarea Philippi, which the Phoenicians call Paneas, springs are shown at the foot of Mount Panius, out of which the Jordan flows. They say that on a certain feast day a victim was thrown in and that through the power of the demon it marvelously disappeared . . . a famous wonder to those who were present. Astyrius was once there when these things were done and seeing the multitude astonished at the affair, he pitied their delusions; and looking up to heaven he supplicated the God over all through Christ that He would rebuke the demon who deceived the people and bring the men's delusion to an end. And they saw that when he prayed thus, immediately the sacrifice floated on the surface of the fountain. And thus the miracle departed and no wonder was ever after performed at the place.

Today on the top of the cliff of Paneas, at the base of which Pan-niches can still be seen, stands the Mohammedan shrine of Sheikh Khudr or Saint George, who is venerated in Moslem as well as in Christian tradition. It takes the place of the temple once erected there by Herod the Great in honor of Caesar Augustus.

In the New Testament the site of Banias, then known as Caesarea Philippi, figures prominently. One day there came there a young Jew named Jesus and his disciples. The little band of Semites must have looked askance at the shrines and temples and palaces with which the source of the river and the often-renamed town were adorned. Slight of figure, bearded and bronzed, they must have drawn their simple cloaks more tightly around themselves in a gesture of dismay and withdrawal. Jesus and his companions were as conscious of beauty as any of their fellow men, but surely those structures devoted to Pan and paganism, to material power and self-glorification and genuflection to Rome were the equivalent of blasphemy in stone against the true intangible and incorporeal divinity of the God of Israel. God could not be captured in blocks of stone nor could as-

35

pects or the essence of His being be represented with the features of mortal man.

As Jesus looked about him in the vainglorious city standing by this source of the Jordan, could not he, familiar as he was with the teachings of Jeremiah, have been recalling the words "Are there any among the false gods of the nations that can bring rain? Or can the heavens give showers? Art thou not he, O Lord our God? We set our hope on thee, for thou doest all these things" (Jeremiah 14:22). Jesus was indeed of the physical race and the spiritual stock of Jeremiah, who spoke in the name of God: "Circumcise yourselves to the Lord; remove the foreskin of your hearts" (Jeremiah 4:4).

In this sense the words of Paul, uttered in accordance with the gospel of Jesus, might have been spoken to the Jews of Jerusalem or of Caesarea Philippi: "For he is not a real Jew who is one outwardly. Nor is true circumcision something external and physical. He is a Jew who is one inwardly, and real circumcision is a matter of the heart, spiritual and not literal" (Romans 2:28, 29). Jesus was also driven by the same prophetic type of compulsion as Amos, who centuries earlier had said: "The Lord God has spoken; who can but prophesy?" (Amos 3:8).

It is in the light of this background that the utterance of Jesus at Caesarea Philippi can best be understood: "Now when Jesus came into the district of Caesarea Philippi, he asked his disciples, 'Who do men say that the Son of Man is?' And they said, 'Some say John the Baptist; some say Elijah; and others Jeremiah, or one of the Prophets.' . . . Simon Peter replied 'You are the Christ, the Son of the Living God' " (Matthew 16:13–16).

Peter's declaration marked a turning point in the life of Jesus. He made up his mind then to go back to Jerusalem, knowing that he might suffer because of his quarrel with unrighteous elders and scribes and priests, and might be executed by the Romans because of his allegedly revolutionary activity against their regime or because of the possible disturbance to public peace so precious to them for the collection of taxes, the conduct of trade and the policing of their far-flung provinces. The exalting motivation of Jesus was in the tradition of the great prophets of Israel. Hosea had declared in the name of God, "For I desire steadfast love and not sacrifice; the knowledge of God, rather than burnt offerings" (Hosea 6:6). Isaiah, among others, had inveighed against exaggerated and senseless ritual and had cried out in the name of God to his people: "Wash yourselves, make yourselves clean; remove the evil of your doings from before my eyes.

Cease to do evil; learn to do good; seek justice, correct oppression; defend the fatherless, plead for the widow" (Isaiah 1:16, 17). None of these men had been afraid of consequences; nor was Jesus. It will be recalled that when Simon Peter attempted to restrain him from following his decision arrived at in Caesarea Philippi, Jesus turned upon him and said: "Get thee behind me, Satan! You are a hindrance to me, for you are not on the side of God but of men" (Matthew 16:23).

AIN LEDDAN

A forty-minute walk west of Banias brings one to the powerful spring of Ain Leddan (the Spring of Dan) that bursts out of the ground to fill two large shallow depressions with swirling pools. They spill into a swift little stream that races like a freshet to form the shortest but strongest of the four sources of the Jordan. It is no surprise to learn that cities were established of old on a low rise in the vicinity of the bountiful spring. Their remains are concealed in the artificial mound of Tell el-Qadi (the Tell of the Judge), as it is called in Arabic. Why the spring retained the Hebrew name of Dan and the tell assumed a related Arabic one is one of the quirks that cannot and need not be explained. The various names mean the same thing—that the "City of the Judge" (i.e., "Dan") is located by the "Spring of Dan," which forms the "River of Dan."

An ancient antecedent name of Tell el-Qadi is remembered in the Bible as being the originally Phoenician-controlled Laish or Leshem (Judges 18:29; Joshua 19:47) before it was changed to Dan. (It is interesting to note that it is mentioned in Egyptian texts as Lus[i].) Located but a short distance north-northwest of Ain Leddan, the long low tree-girt mound of Tell el-Qadi seems at first glance to be nothing more than one of the last outrunners of the nearby chain of hills. The fragments of ancient pottery strewn on its surfaces and around its base testify unmistakably, however, that the site was inhabited long before the tribe of Dan settled there. They furnish clear evidence of occupation as early as the period of Abraham between the twenty-first and nineteenth centuries B.C. Excavations might well reveal that civilized peoples lived there much earlier still, as far back as the prepottery Neolithic period, more than seven millennia ago.

Tell el-Qadi then, identified with Biblical Dan and earlier Laish, today marks the boundary between Syria and Israel. The most thickly inhabited parts of ancient Israel extended between Dan and Beersheba. "From Dan to Beersheba" became a household phrase (I Samuel 3:20; I Kings 4:25). It is supposed to have been quoted by the Bible-bred Welshman Lloyd George to a boundary commission at the Versailles Conference in 1919, when he insisted that the territory of British Mandatory Palestine had to extend as far north as the site of ancient Dan, in accordance with the words of Sacred Writ, and that the boundary line could not be drawn south of it as some of the map-makers had apparently suggested. If the story is not apocryphal, he might also, had he so desired, have quoted another Biblical passage which said in effect that in the heyday of King Solomon's power the territory of Israel extended "from the entrance to Hamath to the Brook of Egypt" (I Kings 8:65), from southern Syria to the dry stream-bed system known today as the Wadi el-Arish that forms a natural north–south geographic boundary through the length of the center of Sinai. But Great Britain wished to keep all of Sinai as a separate entity under its control, letting France have Syria as its share of the war spoils. It would therefore not have been politic for Lloyd George to open up the matter to discussion of Biblical definitions.

NAHR HASBANI

The longest source of the Jordan and the one most directly in line with it is the Nahr Hasbani, which enjoys a life of its own for some twenty-four miles before losing its identity. Starting from an excellent spring at the foot of one of the buttresses of Mount Hermon, it parallels for a considerable distance the lower part of the southern course of the Leontes River (Nahr Litani) to the west. The two streams' parallel southward courses are less than 5 miles from each other until the Leontes turns sharply westward to flow into the Mediterranean.

NAHR BAREIGHIT

The westernmost source of the Jordan is the small mountain stream called the Nahr Bareighit. It is hardly a complimentary name—"the Flea River." Cutting a rude gorge for itself, it tumbles down southward from the hilly meadowland of Merj Ayun, which retains in part its ancient Biblical name Ijon (I Kings 15:20), to enter into the Nahr Hasbani about three quarters of a mile above the point where the Hasbani reaches the junction of the Leddan and Banias streams. These last two alone were once considered the sole sources of the Jordan. All four help create and lose their individual identity in the Jordan as it begins its career under its own name.

I I I / The lake district

The lake that was

After plunging downward over 1000 feet in less than 7 miles, as measured in a straight line from Banias, and trenching its way through basalt country, the newborn Jordan enters the area of the now nearly nonexistent Lake Huleh. Formerly a small triangular body of water spread over much malarial marshland, Lake Huleh has been transformed in recent years by an elaborate series of drainage canals into some 15,000 acres of lush farmland. In its original state it was some 3 miles long, over 2 miles wide at its upper end but narrowing down to a point at the south where the Jordan re-emerged. Its maximum depth was 15 feet. Known to Josephus as Lake Semechonitis, it has for all practical purposes ceased to exist, and the former carefree meanderings of the river through its swamplands and sluggish waters have been reduced to a firmly canalized line.

Fortunately the government of Israel has left an area of several hundred acres of water and swamp at the south end of the former lake and turned it into a wildlife preserve where, to a lesser degree, the fauna and flora for which Lake Huleh was famous continue to flourish. All hunting and fishing are forbidden. Still to be found there are papyrus plants, reeds, bulrushes, high grasses, ferns, water lilies and exotic flowers of many kinds. Jackals, hyenas, some wild boar, among other animals, and all manner of reptiles, land birds and waterfowl continue to make the refuge their permanent or seasonal habitat.

An indelible name

Overlooking the Huleh area from an elevation above its northwest end is the great mound of Tell Abil. It is one of the few sites whose present name still clearly reflects the original Biblical one after the passage of thousands of years, for it was once called Abel-beth-maachah (II Samuel 20:14–15). Both Biblical and archaeological evidence combine with the modern name to make the identification certain. The *Abil* of Tell Abil and the *Abel* of Abel-beth-maachah are undoubtedly one and the same.

There is, however, no reflection whatsoever of a Biblical name in that of Tell el-Qedah, the huge, partly artificial mound located about five miles to the southwest of Lake Huleh. First identified with the great fortified site of Biblical Hazor by John Garstang, who made some soundings there in 1926, its importance stemmed in considerable part from its strategic position astride the trunk highway leading past it from Egypt to Syria, Asia Minor and Mesopotamia.

When more thorough excavations were undertaken there in 1955–1958 under the direction of Yigael Yadin, it became evident that Hazor had been destroyed by the Israelites under Joshua in his Galilean campaign (Joshua 11:10–13) in the thirteenth century B.C. and not, as had been previously thought, a century earlier. It has been estimated that at that time Hazor had a population of some 40,000 and covered an area of some 175 acres, making it the largest inhabited site in the country.

The city mound proper, originally settled in the third millennium B.C., comprised some 25 acres. Immediately north is a massive rectangular enclosure of about 150 acres, with a great dry moat on its west side. This area served as a compound for the chariots and horses of the army of the Hyksos, whose empire from 1700 to 1575 B.C. included Syria, Palestine and Egypt. The great Canaanite city merited the description, as did its Hyksos predecessor, in Joshua 11:10, of once being "the head of all those kingdoms."

The conquest by the Israelites in the thirteenth century B.C. of Hazor,

Bethel, Lachish, Eglon and Debir (Kiriath-sefer) indicates, as G. E. Wright has pointed out, that "during the thirteenth century B.C. a portion at least of the later nation of Israel gained entrance to Palestine by a carefully planned invasion, the purpose of which was not primarily loot but land." This complements the conclusion based on our archaeological explorations of Edom and Moab in southern Transjordan that the Exodus of the Israelites from Egypt (or at least the one featured in the Bible) could not have taken place before the thirteenth century B.C.

"The ambition of nature"

When the modern Israelis canalized the upper Jordan in a straightened and deepened bed, numerous flint and limestone tools and weapons as well as tusks of prehistoric elephants and the remains of other animals were dug up, dating back many thousands of years to eras when a tropical climate prevailed. The Jordan leaves the Huleh area quietly enough and holds itself to a fairly steady pace for about 2 miles. Then, just above Jisr Banat Yaaqub (the "Bridge of the Daughters of Jacob," over which crosses the high-road between Damascus and Galilee, closed now because of political imponderables), the river tears out on a run that for some distance brooks no restraint. It tumbles and cascades through a forbidding, dark-visaged gorge, to emerge at its end foaming and muddy. Somewhat abashed then, it collects itself, wriggles for about another mile through a small plain and delta of its own making to join the clear waters of the Sea of Galilee as if it were a child reaching for its mother. In the distance of about 10 miles between the two points, the Jordan plunges from 230 feet above sea level to 696 feet below, falling almost a hundred feet per mile. The descent from the base of Mount Hermon to the Huleh basin had been even more precipitate.

Thirteen miles long and about 8 miles across at its greatest width, the Sea of Galilee is shaped like a harp, perhaps thereby receiving its ancient name of Kinnereth (Chinnereth), which means just that. Its waters are clear and relatively sweet and at one point more than 150 feet deep. Not only the Jordan but also numerous strong underground springs feed it. One can swim along its shores or farther out in warm waters and suddenly be plunged into an icy bath when passing over an upsurging cold spring. It is still full of fish, mainly caught by fishermen of the State of Israel, in whose territory all of the lake now lies. Hugged by the high hills of Galilee to the west and of the Jaulan to the east, it has for the most part only a very narrow coast. This widens out for a distance of less than 4 miles in the Ghuweir ("Little Valley"), along its northwest shore, which is to be identified with the Biblical land of Gennesaret.

The lava-fed fertility of the shores easily supports a rich tropical vegetation. Israeli colonies have revived intensive agricultural activity around the lake, restoring the green setting which anciently graced it. Bananas, grapes, citrus fruits and vegetables of all kinds, and other crops, are being produced in great quantity, with modern Israeli settlements replacing in number and surpassing in size those that once ringed it, especially in the centuries of Roman control.

The barrenness and desolateness, which, before the modern renaissance brought about by the State of Israel, many a pious pilgrim thought to be a part of historic patrimony, would have been completely unfamiliar to Jesus. He and his disciples often traveled around and across the lake, in connection with which much of importance in his life transpired. A belt of plantations garlanded its shores then, forming the background for some of the fairest towns of the Hellenistic-Roman Near East. There were nine of these towns around the lake. Temples and synagogues, palaces and hippodromes, theaters and bathhouses—all erected in the Graeco-Roman manner—set off this carefully cultivated paradise. Industry thrived. The sound of the carpenter's hammer was common. Hardy fishermen brought home large catches of fish, some of which were then carefully dried and exported to foreign countries. Net-weaving, hide-tanning and boat-building were among other familiar trades. The market places were piled high with an abundance of frequently harvested crops. The merchants traded in goods from far-off places.

Listen to the words of Josephus, a Jewish nobleman who claimed to have been a military governor of Galilee[1] a little more than a generation after the time of Jesus: "Now this lake of Gennesareth is so called from the country adjoining to it. . . . Its waters are sweet and very agreeable for drinking. . . . The lake is also pure and of a temperate nature. . . . The country also that lies over against this lake hath the same name of Gennesareth.

[1] Josephus, *War*, II, 20:3–7.

42

... Its soil is so fruitful that all sorts of trees can grow upon it. ... One may well call this place the ambition of nature. ...["]2

*I*slam triumphant

The Sea of Galilee is visible in wonderful perspective from the heights of Qurun Hattin (the Horns of Hattin), which tower almost 2000 feet above it to the west. They form the top of an extinct volcano that is quite in place among the broad black deposits of basalt in the hills overlooking the lake. Peoples of earliest antiquity knew the Horns and Plains of Hattin. I have picked up there magnificent Palaeolithic flint handaxes belonging to early prehistoric seminomads who grazed their flocks on the top and slopes of the towering hill.

To a much later period belonged the catastrophic battle fought on the waterless heights of Hattin between the Crusaders and the Moslems. It raged from July 2 to July 4, 1187. On the last day the Christian army could no longer stand against the onslaught of Saladin's soldiery. To the burning heat of the sun and the blinding, choking dust raised by the battle was added the scorching southerly wind of a khamsin blowing from the desert. In addition there was a fearful lack of water.

In the valley below, a few scant miles away, could be seen the sparkling blue of the Sea of Galilee. The knights and troops drawn from the fairest lands of Europe had frequently bathed in it, and its cool waters had often quenched their thirst. Now it was nothing more than a miserable mirage, tantalizingly near, unattainably remote, tormenting the pilgrim warriors. How could men fight and human flesh endure when throats were choked with dust and lips were cracked wide open and limbs were leadened beyond the power to move them, all for lack of water? A few of the Crusaders escaped, but most of them were cut down relentlessly by those they themselves would have put to the sword. George Adam Smith writes in this connection: "A militant and truculent Christianity, as false as the relics of the 'True Cross' round which it was rallied, met its judicial end within view of the scenes where Christ proclaimed the Gospel of Peace and went about doing good."[3]

2 *Ibid.*, III, 10:7–8.
3 Smith, *Historical Geography of the Holy Land*, p. 441.

The power of Rome

In honor of an emperor

Much has changed on the shore of the Sea of Galilee during the passage of the millennia, with armies and conflicts receding in memory and serving at best to highlight individuals and ideas whose personalities and significance remain memorable and vital. Almost 2000 years have passed since the little boat in which Jesus and his disciples were seated was tossed about dangerously by one of the sudden tempests that beat the normally calm waters of the Sea of Galilee into raging fury. To his worried disciples Jesus had said: "Why are you afraid, O men of little faith?" (Matthew 8:26).

The power of Rome was paraded around the Sea of Galilee in the time of Jesus. The somber city of Tiberias was its main stronghold. It was founded about A.D. 20 by Herod Antipas, who had inherited the tetrarchy of Galilee and Peraea from his father, Herod the Great. Herod Antipas gave his new capital city the name Tiberias in honor of the emperor Tiberius (A.D. 14–37).

Peopled at first mainly by officials and troops, Tiberias was long shunned by pious Jews because its builders had disturbed an ancient necropolis when laying the foundations. However, the nearness of hot mineral baths to the city lent it growing attractiveness. After the destruction of Jerusalem by the Romans in A.D. 70 it became a great Jewish cultural center. There the Palestine or Jerusalem Talmud was completed in the early Byzantine period, and the Tiberian system of Hebrew pronunciation was developed.

The black ruins of the Roman acropolis that protected the city can still be seen above it. The natural excellence of Tiberias' location has helped preserve it as an inhabited site, although from the scenic point of view it has the least attractive position of any settlement along the entire lake. It is situated on the narrowest part of the lake front, with little green available to relieve its grimness. Even the fine breezes from the west during the summer do not favor it.

Did Jesus shun the place or is it just an accident that it is not mentioned in the Gospels? The Roman troops stationed there were probably frequently moved for relief from its humid heat to camps and cities in the hills of Galilee and Gilead on both sides of the Jordan. Roman legions, sometimes heavy-handed, dominated the life of the times. The prevalent architecture and the most pretentious religious expression were also Roman. Is it to be wondered at that the madman whose troubled spirit Jesus healed called himself by the commonly repeated name Legion? "And Jesus asked him, 'What is your name?' He replied, 'My name is Legion, for we are many'" (Mark 5:9).

The Gadarene swine

Chief among the neighboring Roman hill towns was Gadara, dominating the heights on the east side of the Jordan and directly overlooking from the south the Yarmuk River, which joins the Jordan a few miles south of the Sea of Galilee. It also commands a wonderful view over the Sea of Galilee and its southeast approaches. The extant ruins of this site are of sufficient size and number to enable the visitor to imagine without much difficulty what Gadara looked like in the prime of its existence. The remains of three theaters, a temple, a magnificent colonnaded street, a large reservoir and an aqueduct give an exciting idea of its former grandeur. The ruins of a later Christian basilica can also be made out. Some of the best architectural buildingblocks of Roman and Byzantine structures have been incorporated into the mean houses of the modern Arab village of Umm Qeis at the east end of the earlier town area.

Like its sister city of Gerasa (Jerash) farther south in central Transjordan, whose ruins are much better preserved, Gadara belonged to the union of the cities of the Decapolis in Palestine, Transjordan and Syria that were an ornament to Roman dominion. The name Gadara is best remembered today in connection with the story of the Gadarene swine: "And when he [Jesus] came to the other side of the country of the Gadarenes, two demoniacs met him. . . . They cried out, 'What have you to do with us, O Son of God?' . . . And the demons begged him, 'If you cast us out, send us away into the herd of swine.' . . . And behold, the whole herd rushed down the steep bank into the sea [of Galilee], and perished in the waters" (Matthew 8:28–32).

Curative waters

Far below Gadara, on the north side of the Yarmuk River at the bottom of the gorge marking a natural boundary line between Syria and the Hashemite Kingdom of Jordan to the south, are what may well be the finest and most copious hot springs of the entire Near East. From near and far, people have long sought out their curative waters. An ancient mound at el-Hammeh ("Hot Springs"), as the site is known today, testifies to the presence there of a sophisticated civilized settlement as early as the fourth millennium B.C. It was also called Hamath Geder in the Talmud. I have made soundings there and can testify to the high material culture of its early inhabitants, as illustrated by the excellent pottery they shaped by hand and fired in kilns.

These hot springs, situated only a few miles from the Jordan, may be the ones that figure in the Biblical story of the Syrian leper, Naaman, captain of the host of the king of Syria: "[he] dipped himself seven times in the Jordan, according to the word of the man of God [Elisha]; and his flesh was restored like the flesh of a little child, and he was clean" (II Kings 5:14).

I shall never forget, while bathing there myself one day, suddenly seeing a leper slip into the far end of the same pool I was in. Needless to say, I got out in a hurry, although in the back of my mind I think I was aware of the fact that one could not catch leprosy that way or that quickly.

A sixth-century-A.D. Greek inscription indicates the existence of a special bath for lepers outside Byzantine Scythopolis (Beth-shan) in the direction of the springs southeast of the city. M. Avi-Yonah writes in this connection: "It is possible that there was some connection between the presence of the bath of the lepers at Scythopolis and the river Jordan, in particular the reputed place of baptism at Aenon, several miles south of the town. We know from Gregory of Tours that bathing in the Jordan [following in the footsteps of Naaman] and in particular at the sites of the baptism was regarded as a sovereign cure for leprosy."[4]

The Romans built magnificent bathhouses at el-Hammeh, employing a complicated system of underground channels. They also erected a theater. These celebrated hot springs and baths of Amatha, as the Romans called the place, are mentioned along with Gadara by Strabo: "To Gadara

---

[4] Avi-Yonah, *Israel Exploration Journal*, 13:4 (1963), 325–26.

the pleasure-loving Romans, after having enjoyed the restorative effects of the hot springs, retired for refreshment, enjoying the cooler heights of the city and solacing their leisure with the plays performed in the theaters."

Synagogues

Pictures in mosaics

The remains of a fine synagogue of the Byzantine period have been discovered at el-Hammeh. It is related in general style to the one at Gerasa, where scenes of the Flood story are depicted on a mosaic floor. At Gadara, too, to judge from a basalt building-stone with a menorah (lampstand) carved on it, there was also a synagogue. It seems reasonable to assert that a synagogue existed at almost every Byzantine site of any consequence whatsoever in much of the Fertile Crescent and the entire Mediterranean littoral, with many synagogues of this period replacing those of several centuries earlier. In Palestine proper, they extended from Galilee to the Negev and were a powerful factor in the perpetuation of Judaism long after the temple in Jerusalem had ceased to exist.

The Byzantine synagogue near Tell-es-Sultan at Jericho was oriented toward Jerusalem. As was common to all of the synagogues of the period discovered in Palestine, it was built in the form of a basilica, with a central nave and two lateral aisles. It has a highly decorated mosaic floor with multicolored tesserae in white, red, black, brown and blue. The names of the donors are contained in an Aramaic inscription at one end. In the middle of the mosaic floor is a circular panel showing a seven-branched menorah, a lulab (palm branch) on its left and a shofar (ram's horn) on its right. Beneath is an inscription in Aramaic characters, reading "Peace be upon all Israel." Above this mosaic medallion is a representation of the Torah shrine.

On the mosaic floor of another Byzantine synagogue at Ain Duk (Biblical Naaran), several miles northwest of Jericho, are shown among other things the twelve signs of the zodiac, with their names in Hebrew, encircling the sun chariot. The representation of the zodiac was common in synagogues and churches of the period. In all probability, the same craftsmen introduced the same originally pagan symbols in both the places of worship. In a Byzantine synagogue near Tiberias are depicted on the mosaic floor representations of the seasons of the year as well as pictures of not only nude but also uncircumcised men. This was quite contrary to the attitude that developed at the end of the Byzantine period and thereafter, when representations of pagan symbols as well as of the human form became taboo in synagogue architecture.

Where Jesus preached

About 3 miles southwest of the place where the Upper Jordan empties into the Sea of Galilee lies Capernaum. The present name Tell Hum reflects faithfully the Aramaic one, Kefar Nahum (the Village of Nahum). It is situated close to the lake shore, at the edge of the rich plain of Gennesaret which Josephus so admired.

Capernaum was a border station on the great highway that led from Syria to Palestine. It consequently had a toll post, mentioned in the Gospels. The fame of Capernaum, however, rests particularly upon the fact that Jesus took up temporary abode there after leaving Nazareth. The home of Peter became "the house of Jesus." At Capernaum "... immediately on the Sabbath day he entered the synagogue and taught" (Mark 1:21).

The partly restored ruins of a magnificent successor to this synagogue, built about A.D. 200, can be seen at Capernaum. Constructed in basilica fashion, it was so situated that the worshipers faced toward Jerusalem. The walls were decorated with lovely friezes depicting palms, vines, grapes, acanthus leaves, pomegranates, garlands and mythological creatures, including a seahorse. Among other reliefs were also those of a seven-branched lampstand and the six-pointed star. Also on the walls of the contemporary synagogue at Chorazin, a few miles to the northwest above Capernaum, were sculptured various pagan symbols which, like those at Capernaum, seem to have lost religious significance for the Jews. That applies also in mosaic floors of Byzantine synagogues to the representations of Helios and the sun chariot and the zodiac with its twelve divisions, of the type visible at Beth-Alpha in the Jezreel Plain. Among the Chorazin reliefs were a Medusa and a centaur struggling with a lion. Still other friezes there included reliefs of a man with a staff in his raised right hand and a bunch of grapes in his lowered left hand, and representations of birds, animals and

PRECEDING PAGE: The Jordan
in its lower valley

ABOVE LEFT: The Jordan
winding through its jungle
(Zor) with moonlike hills
extending between it and the
upper part of the Jordan valley

LEFT: Nahr Bareighit, the
westernmost of the sources of
the Jordan

RIGHT: Et-Tannur, place of a
waterfall in the Nahr Bareighit.
S. J. Schweig

ABOVE: Sea of Galilee with
Mount Hermon reflected in it

RIGHT: Main thoroughfare of
Roman Gerasa

PRECEDING PAGE: South Theater
and Forum in Roman Gerasa

ABOVE: Temple of Artemis in
Roman Gerasa

RIGHT: Temple of Artemis,
Gerasa, detail of Corinthian
capitals

58

ABOVE: Crusader castle of Kerak, looking at west side. It occupies the site of the Biblical Qir-hareseth

LEFT: Passageway inside the Crusader castle of Kerak

RIGHT: Detail of inner wall of eighth century A.D. Umaiyad castle at Amman, Jordan

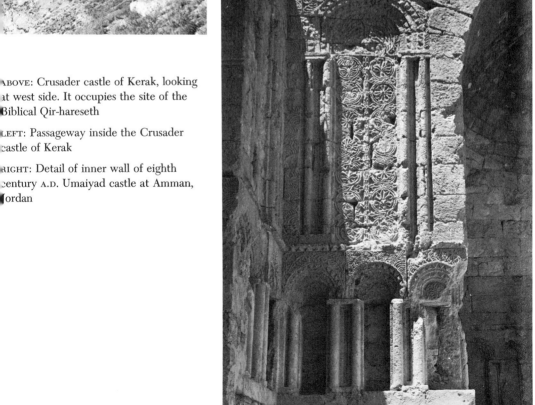

PRECEDING PAGE: Stucco panel of busts from the
eighth century A.D. Umaiyad castle of Khirbet
Mefjer, near Jericho

ABOVE: A magnificent mosaic from the eighth
century A.D. Umaiyad castle of Khirbet Mefjer,
several miles north of Jericho. It shows a stylized
pomegranate (?) tree, with a lion attacking one of
three gazelles grazing underneath its branches. The
border surrounding this brilliantly hued mosaic
gives it a tapestry-like effect. To achieve a sense of
depth, the leaves of the tree are depicted in colors
ranging from leaf green to yellowish green to
blue-gray. The branches and trunk are in various

shades of brown; the animals in shades of pale
yellow to coffee brown; the border in red, white
and black.

RIGHT ABOVE: The Mohammedan shrine of Nebi
Musa (Prophet Moses), on the west side of the
Jordan, with a view toward the Jericho plain

RIGHT BELOW: Qal'at er-Rabad above Ajlun. Built
by one of Saladin's emirs in A.D. 1184, it was
destroyed by Mongol invaders in A.D. 1260, rebuilt
shortly thereafter by Sultan Baybars, and occupied
as late as the nineteenth century A.D. by Ibrahim
Pasha

LEFT: Ancient copper-mine shaft tunnel at Mene'iyeh (Timna). *Nelson Glueck*

BELOW: Monastery of St. George on the left side of the Wadi Qelt, whose waters irrigate the gardens of Jericho. *S. J. Schweig*

64

ABOVE: The great stone tower of the
Pre-Pottery Neolithic A defenses at
Jericho. *Courtesy of Dr. Kathleen M.
Kenyon*

RIGHT: A dolmen in the foothills east
of Tell Damieh (Biblical Adamah) with
an aperture in what was originally a
middle partition

ABOVE: Looking north at the long low mound of el-Qadi, the Biblical Dan, covered with trees and bushes

RIGHT: Unused bricks from brickyard at Tell el-Kheleifeh (Ezion-geber), Solomon's seaport on the eastern arm of the Red Sea. Hidden under debris these sun-dried mud bricks remained intact after an interval of over 2500 years.

FAR RIGHT: Stepped tunnel at Zarethan (Tell es-Sa'idiyeh) with mud-brick wall in the center for dividing the traffic. The pits outside the walls were dug to test the method and date of construction. *Courtesy of Dr. James B. Pritchard, The University Museum*

64

ABOVE: Tombs at Gadara (Umm Qeis)

RIGHT: Underground reservoir at Beit Ras, Jordan, the site of ancient Capitolias

70

ABOVE LEFT: The partly restored ruins of the early synagogue at Capernaum, which probably replaced the one in which Jesus preached

LEFT: The cliff at Banias (Paneas, Caesarea Philippi), with its Pan niches

ABOVE: A Pan niche cut in the face of the cliff at Banias above an artificially hewn cave. Under the niche is a Greek inscription commemorating the god Pan

The Roman theater at Amman, capital of Jordan, also
known as Philadelphia, one of the cities of the Decapolis

plants of various kinds. Dolphin symbols related to the pagan concept of afterlife were carved on a sarcophagus in the third- or fourth-century-A.D. Jewish necropolis of Beth-shearim to the southeast of Haifa. By the same token, the seven-branched lampstand on the head of a relief of a man carved on one of the walls of this underground site makes sense only if it represents the continuity of life after death. It has been shown, indeed, that the menorah on the "Season Sarcophagus" from the Via Appia catacomb in Rome is to be interpreted as a symbol of afterlife.[5]

We read that the people of Chorazin and Capernaum, as well as nearby Bethsaida (Julias), ". . . cities where most of his mighty works had been done," were upbraided by Jesus "because they did not repent" (Matthew 11:20–24). In the synagogue at Chorazin was discovered a stone chair of the type reserved for the most distinguished of the elders of the synagogue. Incised on it was an Aramaic inscription reading "Remembered be for good Judan bar Ishmael, who made this *stoa* and its footstool. As his reward, may he have a share with the righteous." The discovery of this *kathedra* at Chorazin illuminates the passage in Matthew 23:2 that speaks of the "seat of Moses."

"Fisherman's Village"

The banks of the Jordan knew no more storied site than that of Bethsaida— the "Fisherman's Village," to give it a fairly exact translation. Located somewhere almost opposite Capernaum on the northeast side of the Sea of Galilee, it stood perhaps on the east side of the point where the Upper Jordan enters this body of water. Its pattern conformed apparently to that of beautiful Paneas, both of them having been rebuilt by Herod Philip, son of Herod the Great. We read in Josephus: "When [Herod] Philip . . . had built Paneas . . . at the fountains of Jordan, he named it Caesarea. He also advanced the village Bethsaida, situated at the lake of Gennesareth, unto the dignity of a city, both by the number of inhabitants it contained and its other grandeur, and called it by the name of Julias, the same name as the daughter of Caesar [Augustus]."[6]

[5] W. Wirgin, "The *Menorah* as a Symbol of After-Life," *Israel Exploration Journal*, 14:1–2 (1964), 102–4 and Pls. 24 A–C; Goodenough, "The Menorah among Jews of the Roman World," *Hebrew Union College Annual*, XXIII:2 (1950–51), 449–92.

[6] Josephus, *Antiquities*, XVIII, ii, 1.

It was to Bethsaida that Jesus withdrew upon hearing of the beheading of John the Baptist by order of Herod Antipas, who acted upon the insistence of his wife and half-niece Herodias, the mother of Salome (Matthew 14:6–12; Mark 6:22–29). Near Bethsaida is an open area (Mark 6:31–32; Matthew 14:13) thought by some to be the scene of the miracle of feeding the five thousand (Luke 9:10–17).

Loaves and fishes

The ruins of a fine Byzantine basilica commemorating the feeding of the five thousand have been excavated on the southwestern shore of the Sea of Galilee just below Ain Tabghah, between Capernaum and Tiberias. The basilica is now known as the Church of the Multiplication of the Loaves and Fishes, primarily because of the considerable remains of a beautiful mosaic floor dealing with the theme. Built into the altar was a large rough limestone boulder, apparently thought to have been the rock upon which Jesus placed the five loaves and two fishes. Between the altar and the apse is a mosaic showing a basket containing four small round wafers of bread, each marked with a cross. The fifth wafer is not visible. On each side of the basket is a fish. Related bas-reliefs have been found at Byzantine Isbeita in the Negev.

The mosaic floors of the north and south transepts are adorned with pictorial representations of high excellence, equaled in beauty perhaps only by those at Byzantine Beisan, which overlooks the west side of the Jordan some miles south of the Sea of Galilee. In the mosaics of the Church of the Multiplication of the Loaves and Fishes, oleander bushes, rushes, lotus and papyrus plants appear against a light background. Among them can be seen ducks, geese, storks, peacocks, herons and flamingos which seem to be nibbling blossoms or attacking snakes. Smaller birds are visible, too, balancing themselves on branches of trees and/or preening their feathers. Particularly attractive is a pair of birds, placed in a large lotus blossom, caressing one another with their beaks. In the midst of all the colorful flora and fauna are pictures of various buildings, including a Nilometer of the type used originally to measure the rise and fall of the waters of the Nile. Built about 400 A.D., this basilica was repaired later, after damage by earthquake, and was destroyed early in the seventh century A.D. by either the Persians or the Arabs.

Temples of the moon

The preaching of Jesus, like the lessons expounded in the synagogues of his time, was far removed from the pagan religions that had once held sway along the shores of the Sea of Galilee and the banks of the Jordan. The nature of one of these early forms of religion is suggested by the name of an ancient site adjacent to the Jordan River at the point of its emergence as a full-fledged stream from the south end of the Sea of Galilee. The site takes the form of a long low mound called Khirbet Kerak, which has been identified with the Beth-yerah of yore. Archaeological investigation has proven the existence of an advanced agricultural community there near the end of the fourth millennium B.C. and again about the second quarter of the third millennium B.C., not to mention later periods.

The name Beth-yerah means "Temple of the Moon," testifying that already in those early times the cult of the worship of the moon god or goddess was carried on there. This applies also to pre-Israelite Jericho of even greater antiquity, in which name likewise is contained clear intimation of devotion to a lunar deity. From moon worship to worship of one invisible Father of all mankind was a long step forward in the history of human thinking.

I V / "Garden of God"

The present form

At the south end of the Sea of Galilee the Jordan Valley is about 4 miles wide. Pouring out of the lake like a stream from the bottom of a funnel, the river threads its way through the valley, turning first due west and then striking southward along the base of the hills rising above it. Twisting and bending backward sometimes, it runs from side to side like a restless caged animal until it reaches the Dead Sea, in which it loses itself completely. From that immensely deep body of undrinkable water there is no outlet.

The valley through which the river races between the Sea of Galilee and the Dead Sea is 65 miles long and from 3 to 14 miles wide. The river itself bends and reverses direction in quarter- and half- and three-quarter loops to compile an over-all run of some 200 miles. The Jordan Valley falls 590 feet, or an average of about 9 feet a mile in the direct distance between the two bodies of sweet and salt water. It can be understood therefore why, in spite of its pretzel-like configuration within the narrow frame of the lower valley, the current of the Jordan is a swift one. Whirlpools, rapids and small cascades appear frequently along its length. Its constant effort seems to be to gouge ever deeper the geological fault the initial formation of which made the river's appearance inevitable. The fickle stream, endlessly seeking to escape its confines, changes course as often as possible, leaving numerous abandoned bends behind it. From the air they look like skins shed by serpents.

From the Sea of Galilee southward, most of the river proper, in contradistinction to the valley in which it is contained, is about 90 to 100 feet broad and from 3 to 10 feet deep except in springtime, when it is in flood and its waters rise to cover a much wider bed. By the time the Jordan has reached its confluence with the River Yarmuk from the east, at a point approximately five miles south of the Sea of Galilee, it has lost its shining clearness and become muddy as well as turbulent. From then on it has a treacherous zigzag current, tearing from one side to the other and bent apparently upon undercutting and dumping into the Dead Sea as much of the earth on the sides of its banks as it possibly can.

History has magnified the Jordan out of all proportion to its actual size. Its basic importance cannot be exaggerated; its role in the annals of humanity has been great beyond all rational measurement. This statement applies also to Palestine, which is no larger than New Hampshire or Vermont and considerably smaller than Switzerland. Like the Jordan River in particular, the Holy Land in general must be considered in a unique category. It combines everything from the temperate to the tropical, from high hills to the lowest valley in the world, from the white snows of Mount Hermon that replenish the sources of the Jordan to the dark acridity of the Dead Sea in which it is drowned. It is a land of excitement and extremes, of fierce light and sudden darkness, of ecstatic fulfillment and incomprehensible effacement. The deepening appreciation of God insofar as we comprehend Him today has been its most glorious achievement.

"Jungle of the Jordan"

The actual bed of the present Jordan River is contained within a floodplain known in Arabic as the Zor ("Thicket"), which in turn is contained within a higher, much broader and largely cultivable plain known in Arabic as the Ghor ("Depression"). At floodtime in the spring, the Jordan escapes the confines of its actual bed to frolic in the lower floodplain (the Zor), which is from two hundred yards to a mile wide. Unlike that of the Nile, however, the Jordan's annual flood leaves no blessing of silt deposited in its wake. The overflowing Jordan carries away at least as much earth as it leaves behind, and it litters the banks of the Zor with debris.

This narrow floodplain through which the Jordan slices its uninhibited way is tropical and for the most part lush green in color. Its vegetation is rank, and thorns and thistles grow shoulder-high. Dense and at times almost impenetrable thickets of oleander, cane, tangled bushes, vines, willows, poplars and twisted tamarisks beset the traveler's way. The lush growth stands out all the more startlingly because of the desert-white and dark gray of the "Lisan" sediment slopes which confine it. In Biblical times, this Thicket of the Jordan was known as *ge'on hay-yarden*, the "Jungle of the Jordan." (The phrase was formerly incorrectly translated as the "Pride of the Jordan," because of a misunderstanding of the significance of the root of the word in Biblical Hebrew.) And a very good name "Jungle" was. Lions had their lairs there, and it is still frequented by jackals and sometimes wolves. The Bible reads: "Behold, like a lion coming up from the Jungle of the Jordan against the strong sheepfold . . . " (Jeremiah 49:19). We can also now better understand Jeremiah 12:5: "And if in a safe land you fall down, how will you fare in the Jungle of the Jordan?"

At one place in the Zor or Jungle, where the Jordan makes a three-quarter bend around a fertile strip of flatland, bounded on the east by the hillocks rising to the higher level of the Jordan Valley, is a little hidden paradise with several springs of its own. The small artificial mound at its center marks the existence of an ancient settlement. We were able to determine from fragments of pottery on its slopes and around its base that it belonged to the times of the kings of Israel and Judah. Whence came and whither disappeared the small number of inhabitants who tilled the soil of this lonely place, cut off from all except occasional and difficult contact with the outside world? Was it pressure of population or a particular community of interests that brought them to this secluded nook? Today it is called el-Meqbereh, "Burial Place," and is visited infrequently by seminomadic Arabs to bury their dead.

*T*he valley proper

Different levels

When most people talk about the Jordan Valley, they are really thinking of its upper level, the Ghor ("Depression"), not of its lower one, the Zor

("Thicket"). There is as much as 150 feet difference in height between them. Separating them and marking the transition from the one to the other are grotesquely ragged, grayish marl hills of "Lisan" sediments called *qattarah* in Arabic, on which practically nothing grows or ever has grown. One may say that there are three terraces, with two steep slopes between them, leading down to the Jordan River, whether one approaches it from the highlands of Palestine to the west or of Transjordan to the east. First come the broken plateaus or hill country of Palestine and Transjordan, then the steep jagged descent to the Jordan Valley proper (the Ghor), from which in turn desert-dead hills lead down to the Jungle of the Jordan. It is in this Zor that the river weaves its frenzied pattern.

The name most commonly employed in the Bible to describe the main or Ghor part of this upper bench of the Jordan Valley is *kikkar hay-yarden*, as distinguished from the narrower and lower Zor part, *ge'on hay-yarden*, the "Jungle of the Jordan." The existence of these two distinctive levels of the Jordan Valley is described in Lynch's *Official Report of the United States Expedition to Explore the Dead Sea and the Jordan River:* "There are evidently two terraces to the Jordan, and through the lowest one the river runs its serpentine course.... Above the immediate banks,... on each side [is] a singular terrace of low hills, like truncated cones, which is the bluff terminus of an extended table land." This "extended table land" is to be identified with the Biblical *kikkar hay-yarden,* literally "Encircled Jordan Valley." This name applies also to separate parts, with some sections referred to variously as *emeq* ("deep valley"), *biqah* ("opening out" or "fissure") or *arabah* ("plain").

What Lot saw

The immediate and most apparent reasons for the prosperity of the Jordan Valley in ancient times are its strategic location, exuberantly rich earth and abundance of water, which, to be sure, is not evenly distributed. The valley is a great catchment basin, gathering not only the waters of the snows of Mount Hermon and of seasonal rains but also of the tributary streams reaching it from the east and west, which tap thousands of square miles of runoff areas in the broken plateau lands above it. It is amazing to see how the thirsty valley opens up wide to receive these branches with their perennial streams. It fairly unfolds to be made fruitful by them. For a distance of some 13 miles, starting from the Sea of Galilee, the valley is little more and sometimes less than four miles wide. Where the Jalud stream descends through the plain of Beth-shan (Beisan) on the west side to empty into the Jordan River, the valley throws its arms around it, as if to say "Welcome, my beloved." Here the valley is from six to seven miles across. Soon, however, the starved hills of Samaria press in severely to break the embrace. They practically trample upon the floor of the valley, which perforce pulls itself together and narrows down to slender proportions.

Farther south, again on the west side, the Wadi Farah cleaves its way through the austere hills and forces them to retreat. Relieved of their presence and pressure, the Jordan Valley elbows its way into a space 8 miles wide. It continues then to expand as it grows longer, so that by the time it reaches the Jericho district, where it is further enriched by the strong flow of the Wadi Qelt coming from the west, it has achieved its maximum width of 14 miles.

The nature of the Jordan Valley is clearly suggested in the Bible. "And Lot lifted up his eyes and saw that the entire Jordan Valley was irrigated, . . . and it was like a garden of God" (Genesis 13:10). Lot may frequently have been wrong in the eyes of his inquisitive wife, who apparently could not refrain from keeping on looking backward, but he was certainly right in his appreciation of the Jordan Valley. The Biblical description may have been directed especially to the southern part of the valley, particularly to the rich Jericho region and to the well-watered Plains of Moab extending down to the northeast end of the Dead Sea, but it applies equally well to much, although not to all, of the rest of its length as far as the Sea of Galilee. It can now be stated on the basis of painstaking archaeological exploration and excavation that the Jordan Valley was not only the first and oldest settled and farmed area of the Holy Land and perhaps of the entire world, but that it may also have been the richest and most prized part of the Land of Promise. The conquest of its oldest and most fateful city, Jericho, was physically and spiritually compulsory for the Israelites of the Exodus. Human hands and hearts, however, more than water and soil and strategic location, have always ultimately determined whether or not the Valley of the Jordan could be designated a Garden of God.

Roads through the Jordan Rift
From the Dead Sea to Dan

It was through the Jordan Valley, in all probability, that Abram, later to become known as Abraham, pursued and caught up with the kidnapers of Lot, who had fled with much booty of captives and goods when Sodom and its sister cities fell before the onslaught of the kings of the east headed by Chedorlaomer of Elam. The chase was fast and far. Not until he and his followers got to Dan by one of the sources of the Jordan, the Nahr Leddan, could battle be joined with the enemy. "So the enemy [Chedorlaomer and his confederates] took all the goods of Sodom and Gomorrah, and all their provisions. . . . They also took Lot . . . who dwelt in Sodom, and his goods, and departed. Then one who had escaped came and told Abram the Hebrew, who was living by the Oaks of Mamre [in Hebron]. . . . When Abram heard that his kinsman had been taken captive, he led forth his trained men, born in his house, 318 of them, and took up pursuit as far as Dan. And he divided his forces against them by night, he and his servants, and routed them and pursued them to Hobah, north of Damascus. Then he brought back all the goods, and also brought back his kinsman Lot, with his goods and the women and the people [taken captive]" (Genesis 14:11–16).

The raiders, traditionally striking as far from home as possible and then disappearing after a hit-and-run attack, suffered a painful surprise. The reaction and pursuit had been far swifter and more forceful than they had figured on. They were struck hard before they had opportunity to disperse and to dispose of their gains. The dynamic sheikh Abram had lost little time in his encampment under the oak trees of Mamre by Hebron after news of the disaster had reached him. Harm done to any of his group was his own hurt. Gathering together all his effectives, a rapidly moving band of 318 fighting men, he sped to rescue and revenge.

I believe this number to be exactly correct, although aware of the fact that it had to be transmitted orally from father to son for well over a thousand years before the incident could possibly have been committed to writing. Even today there are old men in the tents of Arabia who can recite the history of their ancestors for many generations, and if in their recital they stray a jot from the facts, others within hearing will immediately correct them or supply forgotten details.

If, as we have assumed, Abram's pursuit led to Dan through the Jordan Valley, or at least partway through the Jordan Valley, he followed tracks well known to him. He who was famous for his open-handed hospitality would not lack a welcome wherever he turned. Even if he had been a complete stranger, he would, because of the rules of hospitality, have been received with open arms, although a band of the size that accompanied him would have had to take its own food supplies along. Detailed information as to the path of flight of the raiders would readily have been furnished by eyewitnesses along the way.

Time and again my onetime companion in archaeological expeditions, Rashid Hamid, and I have halted our horses in the late afternoon in front of a chieftain's tent after completing a day of archaeological exploration in the Jordan Valley, almost always to find that knowledge of our presence in the area and of the probability of our coming to a particular place had preceded us. Invariably some of the men seated in the tent would run out, grasp the reins and beg us to dismount and stay with them. Even before we had entered the shade of their "house of hair" a happy bustle would ensue. Mattresses would be spread out, rugs laid, camel saddles moved into position to rest on while reclining, the coals of the fire stirred to prepare coffee and tea, and a few hours later a bounteous meal would be served.

Did not Abram-Abraham himself act thus to unknown wayfarers? "As he sat at the door of his tent in the heat of the day, he lifted up his eyes and looked, and behold, three men stood in front of him. When he saw them, he ran from the tent door to meet them and bowed himself to the earth and said, 'Let a little water be brought, and wash your feet, and rest yourselves under the tree, while I fetch a morsel of bread, that you may refresh yourselves, and after that you may pass on.' . . . So they said, 'Do as you have said.' . . . And Abraham hastened into the tent to Sarah and said, 'Make ready quickly three measures of fine meal, knead it and make cakes.' And Abraham ran to the herd and took a calf, tender and good, and gave it to the servant, who hastened to prepare it. . . . He set it before them and he stood by them under the tree while they ate" (Genesis 18:1–8).

It may well be that Abram and his company of warriors tarried hardly at all during their pursuit of the enemy. They could easily have filled their saddlebags with provender sufficient for their slender needs for several days. I journeyed once with an Arab camal train for thirteen successive days in the wild desert of the Wadi Arabah south of the Dead Sea. Barren and empty, lacking even water except for a few meager springs at infrequent intervals, it was then a formidable area to traverse even on a camel. My companions and I had for food a sack of flour and the grudgingly yielded milk of a female camel. Every night we baked unleavened bread in hot ashes, after the fashion of the Israelites of the Exodus.

From Elath to Sodom

It is surprising what distances can be traversed if beasts and riders are hard-pushed. One night the then Assistant British Resident of Transjordan, Hugh M. Foot (later to be knighted and become Governor of Cyprus), several Arab companions and I, riding on camels, left Aqabah, the seaport of the Wadi Arabah. We were headed northward for the south end of the Dead Sea, some 110 miles away. By the time we had loaded our camels, darkness had snuffed out the day, bringing quick blackness. We mounted and rode northward by the light of a full moon shining brightly in cloudless dry skies. The camels stepped out protestingly. But camels are the most confirmed pessimists and grumblers I have yet met. No matter what you do with them they grumble. If you shift your weight in the saddle, they grumble. If you make them kneel, they grumble. If you tap them on their long necks with the driving cane to quicken their pace, they grumble. Despite all their grumbling, they are marvelous beasts for desert journeys.

We were five men and five camels all told. With us rode Sheikh Audeh ibn Jad, the head of the Injadat Arabs who live on the Transjordan side of the Wadi Arabah. The Injadat Arabs are thought by some to be the descendants of the ancient Gadites, one of the two and a half tribes comprised of Reuben, Gad and half the tribe of Manasseh that settled on the east side of the Jordan. Whether or not Audeh ibn Jad was truly a lineal descendant of the Gadites is highly doubtful. He was, however, a perfect gentleman, a born leader and a splendid companion, full of wit and wisdom, who knew how to find his way unerringly in the then largely unmapped wastes of the Wadi Arabah. Abraham may well have looked like him.

The night grew and peace settled over us as we rode. We watched the evening stars peep over the hills of Edom, then with mounting boldness climb high into the heavens. The moon lighted our way with indefatigable brilliance. Sometimes we rode five abreast and then again in single file. I thought of the ancient Israelites, who trekked north with their Kenite companions along the Bedouin path we were following to the watered site of Punon (modern Feinan), on the east side of the Arabah. The Bible tells us they camped there in the course of their wanderings from Sinai to the Promised Land (Numbers 33:42).

The hours lengthened and the cold penetrated our tightly hugged cloaks. These were Arab *abayas* of hand-woven woolen cloth, little different in all probability from those once used by Abraham and his men. After five hours or so in the saddle, we decided to call a brief halt. The camels were made to couch so that we could dismount and were given a feed of barley, which they grumblingly accepted. A bright fire of dry brush was lit and some hot broth prepared; it tasted like nectar. We snatched a few brief hours of sleep. Soon we mounted again, shaken to complete wakefulness as the camels lurched drunkenly to standing position and then swayed forward with long-paced steadiness like a rising and falling ship breasting the waves. Dawn broke, the sun rose, first to warm and then to roast us. All day long we rode, making only the briefest of stops at long intervals. When the day was done, half the trip was over. We pushed on. Another night and most of another day, and by evening's fall the second day we had reached our goal at the southern end of the Dead Sea, only a little the worse for wear.

In such wise Abraham and his men may have dashed by forced marches from Hebron to the north end of the Dead Sea and then along the Jordan Valley to waylay and discomfit the raiders, who were overtaken finally at its northern end at Dan. Records do not reveal whether or not Abraham and his company tarried along the way, although it may be presumed that they were hospitably received wherever they made a brief halt. Suffice it to say that in his time, near the beginning of the second millennium B.C., there were numerous settlements both large and small on both sides of the Jordan Valley. Many of their inhabitants lived for part of the year in oval or more-or-less circular stone houses and employed well-baked handmade pottery of a distinctive nature. It was their habit to dwell for months in tents, which they shifted periodically from site to site, and to reserve their stone villages as home bases and storage places, as many Arabs do today. Still others dwelt then, as considerable numbers do in modern times, under tent roofs the year round, moving their camping spot seasonally in accordance with varying agricultural and grazing needs.

*T*he springtime of Israel

In the springtime of Israel, the Tent of Testimony was considered to be the sanctuary of the Lord. Later it was to be displaced by the Phoenician-style temple of Solomon. The simplicity of the tent is sweet to the heart of the unspoiled Semite and the life and social organization that go with it are preferred to much treasure. Kings and palaces and permanent stone houses are repugnant to them. With crystal clairvoyance the prophet Samuel portrayed the evil possibilities of earthly kings when presenting his objections to the appointment of one of them over the people of Israel, who insisted upon being like the other nations.

It is written that Samuel said: "These will be the ways of the king who will reign over you: he will take your sons and appoint them to his chariots and to be his horsemen . . . and some to plow his ground, and to reap his harvest, and to make his instruments of war. . . . He will take your daughters . . . and . . . your fields and your vineyards and your olive groves . . . and in that day you will cry out because of your king . . ." (I Samuel 8:11–18).

More extreme even than Samuel in recalling the Israelites to their Spartan beginnings were the Rechabites. These ascetic folk were closely related in habit and thought to some of the early prophets of Israel, who initiated the tendency to idealize the pristine days in the desert. The Rechabites followed the precept of their founder: "Jonadab the son of Rechab, our father, commanded us saying, 'You shall not drink wine, . . . nor sow seed; you shall not plant or have a vineyard; but you shall live in tents all your days, that you may live many days in the land wherein you so-journ' " (Jeremiah 35:6–7).

It is no accident that Rechabite doctrines were in harmony with the teachings and activities of Elijah and Elisha, in whose lives the Jordan figured so prominently. Nor is it strange that the later Essenes, to whose philosophy John the Baptist may have been attracted, had much in common with them.

Philo says of the Essenes: "Among all men, they alone are without money and without possessions, but are nevertheless the richest of all, because to have few wants and to live frugally they regard as riches. Among them is no maker of any weapons of war, . . . nor do they follow any occupation that leads to injustice and covetousness."[1] Many of these humble and modest Essenes, whose influence upon earliest Christianity was large, were at home in the Jordan Valley, particularly in the neighborhood of Jericho, while some of them apparently settled at Qumran in the hills overlooking the northwest end of the Dead Sea. They may have penned the Dead Sea Scrolls discovered there and in the nearby Wadi Murabaat, as well as the intimately related documents found in the Cave of Letters in the Nahal Hever close to Ain Gedi and in the excavations of the great Judaean fortress of Masada, all of which sites are located above the west side of the Dead Sea.

[1] Philo, *Quod Omnis Probus Liber Sit*, Art. 12.

V / Canyons from the east

The Yarmuk

The streams on the east side of the Jordan and of the Dead Sea are more numerous and generally larger than those on the west side. The tips of their branches commence far to the east at the line separating the Desert from the Sown. Gathering strength from numerous sources, they slash their way deeply across the high and broken Transjordanian plateau, severing it into distinctive segments. Steep canyons that level down and out when they reach the valley of the Jordan mark their cross-country runs.

Between the Sea of Galilee and the Sea of Salt eleven perennial streams come from the east to swell the flood of the Jordan. They water its valley into the greenness which drew from Lot the exclamation that it was "like a garden of God." Their names may sound strange to the unaccustomed ear, but water spells music and wealth in any language. From north to south, they are now called the Yarmuk, Arab, Ziqlab, Jurm, Yabis, Kufrinji, Rajeb and Zerqa, followed some 16 miles farther south by the Nimrin, the Kefrein and the Rameh (Hesban), the latter two joining before emptying into the Jordan. Beyond them is the small Wadi Azeimeh whose outlet is at the northeast corner of the Dead Sea.

Of these eleven streams, the main ones emptying into the Jordan from the east are the Yarmuk in the north, the Zerqa in the center and the

Hesban-Rameh in the south. Below them are the great canyons of the Mojib and the Hesa, which empty into the Dead Sea. With the exception of the Hesban-Rameh, these larger perennial streams are known by name in the Bible and figure frequently in its accounts. The Yarmuk still retains its ancient Biblical name. The Wadi Zerqa is the Biblical Nahal Jabboq, the Wadi Mojib is the Biblical Nahal Arnon and the Wadi Hesa is the Biblical Nahal Zered. All of them are smaller than the Jordan with the exception of the Yarmuk. When the latter two come together, they meet on almost equal terms so far as volume is concerned.

Commencing in the eastern desert, the Yarmuk flows westward through a canyon grim with volcanic blackness to pour into the Jordan at a point about four miles south of the Sea of Galilee. It brings to the Jordan nearly as great a quantity of water as the Jordan itself possesses at this point, both of them being thirty feet broad at their confluence. If somewhat less in volume, the waters of the Yarmuk are sweeter than those of the Jordan. They have been tapped in modern times by the Hashemite Kingdom of Jordan for irrigation purposes in the Jordan Valley to an extent never previously known.

The Yarmuk forms a natural boundary line between modern Syria and the Hashemite Kingdom of Jordan; in ancient times it separated Syria from north Gilead. Extending on both sides of the Yarmuk in Biblical times was the territory of the fabulous Og, king of Bashan. He was the last of the Rephaim (Giants), according to the Bible. It informs us that he and Sihon, the other king of the Amorites, between them ruled the territory east of the Jordan extending from the River Arnon (Wadi Mojib, which empties into the middle of the Dead Sea) as far as Mount Hermon far to the north of the Yarmuk River. After Og's death, legend has it that his gigantic bed was placed on exhibition at Rabbath Ammon, where it was viewed with wonder by sightseers. "His [Og's] bedstead was a bedstead of iron; is it not [on display] in Rabbah of the Ammonites? Nine cubits was its length and four its breadth, according to the common cubit" (Deuteronomy 3:11).

We are told furthermore that Og had two residences, one in Ashtaroth and the other at Edrei (Deuteronomy 1:4). The first is on the north and the second on the south side of the broken highlands bordering the Yarmuk gorge. Ashtaroth, abandoned for millennia, may be identified with Tell Ashtarah, as Albright has pointed out, and Edrei with modern Derah, today an important railway junction. Edrei or Derah has apparently been occupied more or less continuously for at least five thousand years. Among its wonders is a complete subterranean city belonging mainly to Roman and Byzantine times. The wadi or stream-bed below it drains into the Yarmuk, whose waters are fed by a considerable number of tributaries rising in southern Syria and northern Gilead.

Arab gateway

It was through the Yarmuk gorge that the Arab forces cascaded down into the Jordan Valley after overwhelming the army of the Byzantine emperor Heraclius at the famous Yarmuk battle in A.D. 636. They soon overcame all of Syria, Palestine and Egypt. Retreating after that to the serenity of theological speculation, Heraclius made no further effort to stem the advancing tide of martial Islam. Like a raging freshet tearing through a dry stream-bed, this Arab flood swept away almost every obstacle in its path. Jerusalem opened its gates to the Caliph Omar in A.D. 637, and the Caesarea Maritima that Herod the Great had once built as a glittering city and seaport on the west coast of Palestine was conquered in 640. A new era ensued, in the beginning beneficent and brilliantly creative.

UMAIYAD UNDERTAKINGS

The Umaiyad and Abbasid caliphs brought many blessings to the entire Near East. They were among the very last for a long time in that part of the world who paid careful attention to the cultivation of the soil, to the building of terraces to prevent soil erosion and to the repair and construction anew of dams, reservoirs, aqueducts and cisterns. From their predecessors, whom they largely absorbed, they learned much, soon imparting to everything to which they put their hands and hearts the elan and imprint of their own constructive dynamism. Seemingly, most of the pagan Nabataeans, themselves of Semitic stock, who had become Christianized in the early Byzantine period and whose artistic influence is clearly visible in early church art in the Negev and elsewhere, now became fervent Moslems. As such they contributed the protracted memories and enterprising spirit of their own enduring cultural traditions to the emerging cultural patterns of the new conquerors.

What better tribute to the architectural accomplishments of these sophisticated Umaiyads can there be, for example, than the breathtaking Dome of the Rock (the so-called Mosque of Omar in Jerusalem), built in

A.D. 691 by the Umaiyad prince Abd el-Malik with the aid of Greek Christian architects and workmen; and also the Mosque el-Aqsa there, transformed in the seventh century A.D. by the Moslems from the basilica of St. Mary built by Emperor Justinian in 536.

And who has not been amazed by the beauty of the hunting lodges erected in the eastern deserts of Transjordan by pleasure-loving Umaiyad princes to help them wile away pleasant weeks of sophisticated leisure during the spring of the year? To an opulent desert retreat such as Qeseir Amra they could return after a day's hunting and further amuse themselves with recitals of poetry and speculations about astronomy, as well as with wine, women and song. The enjoyment of these diversions could only have been heightened for them by contrast with the austerity of the desert. The Islamic prohibitions against drinking and wenching had not yet become the order of the day. Reclining on their couches, appetites comfortably sated, they could gaze at ceilings decorated with paintings of voluptuous nudes and of dancing bears playing musical instruments.

The ruins of a beautiful Umaiyad structure are still visible in Amman, and the remains of the great Umaiyad complex of Qasr el-Heir el-Gharbi testify to the strength of the Umaiyad presence in Syria. On the northwest shore of the Sea of Galilee the ruins of an Umaiyad castle have been discovered at Khirbet Minyeh. And a most elaborate winter palace, begun and brought nearly to completion by the Umaiyads, has been excavated at Khirbet Mefjer, three miles north of Jericho. An earthquake seems to have destroyed it in the middle of the eighth century A.D., before the building could be finished. Its dimensions and general plan, as well as its sculptures and decorations, reveal Umaiyad capabilities to high advantage. The reliefs, statues and ornamentation of all kinds show clearly the indirect influence of the Hellenistic-Semitic art of their earlier Nabataean predecessors. The Umaiyads thus take their prideful place among the long line of those who have influenced the course of events and the development of civilization in the Jordan Valley.

Enterprise in the desert

Standing at the edge of the fertile plateau of North Gilead and looking down into the depths of the mighty chasm of the Yarmuk, one would scarcely count on finding any ancient settlements on its precipitous slopes or along its narrow banks. So compelling, however, has population pressure been in the lands bordering the inhospitable wastes of the Arabian desert, intensified by constant migration from that perpetually hungry land itself, that no possibly cultivable area in the ancient Near East has been left untouched in one period or another of history. Even marginal lands were made arable by dint of almost incredible effort and ingenuity. In hard-headed terms of capital investment and income return, as such things are reckoned today, the cost of establishing a village on one of the sides or at the bottom of the Yarmuk gorge, or in regions even less favorable for human settlement such as the Wadi Arabah or the Negev, would seem hopelessly impractical. But the ancients never calculated that way. They emphasized survival values which cannot be figured in the terms of the modern market place. Otherwise, such comparatively formidable dams as the Romans built in the eastern desert of Transjordan in places like the Wadi Dhobai, or such elaborate terraces looking like gigantic checkerboards as the Nabataeans constructed in the midst of the wastes of the Wadi Arabah at a place like et-Telah could never possibly have been built.

Visit the forbidding lands of northernmost Transjordan, for instance, and gaze at a whole series of ruins of once-flourishing Nabataean-Roman-Byzantine towns, where today practically no sedentary civilized life stirs at all. Each town had several large reservoirs, and almost every house had a covered cistern hewn for the most part out of solid rock and measuring on the average 10 feet square and deep. The sight of the massive ruins of stone-built towns and villages in this area between the Iraq Oil Company's east–west pipeline and the Syrian border to the north of it, such as Umm el-Jemal, Sabkhah, Deir el-Kahf, Umm el-Qetein and Burqaah leave one filled with amazement at what men can accomplish when peace and vision, planning and diligence, mutual need, common decency and brotherly cooperation prevail. To those who escape from the penury of the desert, the labor and sweat of tilling the soil are of little moment compared to the larger amount of food and general betterment in living conditions obtained.

It is not unnatural that the site of Gadara, one of the fairest cities of the Decapolis, should have been located near the edge of the fertile plateau of Gilead, bordering the southern top of the Yarmuk canyon. It was unexpected, however, to find even along the Yarmuk's steep slopes and at its bottom the remains of ancient villages or hamlets, large and small, dating from the beginnings of civilization to the end of the medieval Arabic period.

Near the outlet of the Yarmuk into the Jordan, in the fertile valley between the junction of the two rivers, Moshe Stekelis unearthed a Pottery Neolithic settlement at Shaar ha-Golan, belonging to the third quarter of the fifth millennium b.c. Albright dates the settlement between circa 4500–4250 b.c. and places it in historical sequence in the gap of history that occurs between the Early Pottery Neolithic of Jericho IX and the Late Pottery Neolithic of Jericho VIII.

All these tattered fragments of former achievements testify eloquently to man's creative ability and productive attachment to the soil on the one hand, and on the other to his demonic compulsion to tear down in a day what others have constructed in many generations of labor.

River Jabbok (Wadi Zerqa)

South of the Yarmuk River, the next largest stream entering the Jordan from the east is the Nahal (River) Jabbok, known today as the Wadi Zerqa. It rises at a spring in Amman, the capital of the Hashemite Kingdom of Jordan. Rabbath Ammon was the city's full name of old, when it was the capital of the kingdom of Ammon. Mute witness of spent glory are the ruins of a Roman theater, built when the town's name was changed in the Hellenistic-Roman period to Philadelphia (City of Brotherly Love). The native inhabitants of the land and their descendants during nearly a millennium continued, however, to call it by its old name. It was restored to official usage when the flood of Islam swept away not only the power of Byzantium with its Hellenistic-Roman traditions but also as many of its trappings and forms and designations as possible. A consciously archaizing tendency came to the fore. Semitic names which had been lurking in the background of stubborn memory for many centuries were refurbished and placed on the signposts of common usage. Many of the Greek appellations were intentionally abandoned and frequently became totally forgotten.

At first the Jabbok flows north for some miles and then turns and pursues a constant course westward through a descending valley narrowing into an ever-deeper canyon. Finally its high and steep walls drop away suddenly to a rich plain which merges with the Jordan Valley. In it are ancient cities, most of whose former names have been completely forgotten. Two of them, Succoth and Adamah, are mentioned in the Bible. Adamah is to be identified with Tell Damieh. Succoth is to be identified with Tell Deir-alla. Other Biblical sites in the Jordan Valley are also referred to in the Biblical narrative, such as Zarethan, Zaphon, Jabesh-gilead, Beth-shan and Jericho, but still only a comparative few of the dozens that we found in the course of our archaeological explorations are mentioned. Here again we observe the highly selective choices of places, people and events by the Biblical editors, treating only those that best fitted the overriding moral-religious exposition and historical-theological purpose of the Bible as a whole.

South and North Gilead

The initial south–north line of the Jabbok River served as a boundary line between the small Ammonite kingdom to the east and part of the territory of Sihon, king of the Amorites, to the west, before Sihon's territory was taken over by the Israelites. The continuing east–west course of the Jabbok formed the boundary between South Gilead and North Gilead. North Gilead comprises the territory between the Yarmuk and Jabbok rivers and South Gilead the territory south of the Jabbok as far as the great canyon of the Arnon River (Wadi Mojib) that empties into the middle of the east side of the Dead Sea. South Gilead may be equated with the kingdom of the Amorites ruled over by Sihon, whom the Israelites conquered and whose territory was settled then by the two tribes of Reuben and Gad (Numbers 32:33; Deuteronomy 3:12).

Originally, Sihon's kingdom extended southward from the Jabbok only as far as the Wadi Hesban, which, combining the waters of the Wadi Ramah and the Wadi Kefrein, is the southernmost of the eastern tributaries of the Jordan. When the Israelites entered Transjordan they found that the Amorites under Sihon had extended their kingdom southward to the Arnon (Wadi Mojib) by taking over the original northern part of the Moabite kingdom contained between the Wadi Hesban and the Arnon. At the time of the Exodus, the Moabite kingdom was restricted thus to the area between the Arnon and the Zered (Wadi Hesa) to the south.

The "Rest of Gilead" or North Gilead, between the Jabbok and the Yarmuk rivers, and the district of Bashan to the north of the Yarmuk belonged originally to the kingdom of Og, and was assigned, after it had been conquered by the Israelites, to half of the tribe of Manasseh (Deuteronomy 3:13; Joshua 13:30, 31).

Little wonder that Moses was concerned over the request of Reuben, Gad and half of Manasseh to remain behind and settle in the good lands of pine-clad South and North Gilead while the rest of the tribes moved westward across the Jordan into the Promised Land. The great canyons of these streams and of the Zered still farther south split the other side of the Jordan into geographically self-contained wholes. The rivers served thus both as barriers and boundaries to the highlands above them.

The cities of the Jordan Valley such as Jericho, Beth-shan and Jabesh-gilead were, to be sure, not completely cut off from their highland sisters. Part of the importance of these cities lay in their location astride the few available roads that lead across the Jordan Valley from one broken plateau to another on either side of it. The fact remains, however, that most of the inhabitants of the Jordan Valley never stirred out of it. Nor did their neighbors from the heights above have much occasion to see or interest in knowing the Jordan Valley. By the same token, Moses could foresee that if the two and a half tribes of Israel settled in distinctively separated segments of the land on the east side of the Jordan Rift, they would lose their closeness of relationship with the communities of their brethren on the west side of it in the Land of Canaan proper.

What effect would the separation caused by the Jordan Valley have upon the continued unity of the tribal federation? Already these would-be secessionists had said to Moses: "Bring us not over the Jordan" (Numbers 32:5). And he had sharply replied: "Shall your brethren go to war while you sit here? Will the result not be to discourage the heart of the children of Israel from going over into the land which the Lord has given to them?" (Numbers 32:6, 7). They replied reassuringly: "Let us build sheepfolds here [in South and North Gilead] for our flocks and cities for our children. We ourselves will be ready to go armed before the children of Israel until we have brought them to their place. . . . We will not return to our houses until . . . every single Israelite will come into his inheritance. For we will not inherit with them on the other [west] side of the Jordan; because our inheritance has come to us on this side of the Jordan eastward" (Numbers

32:16–19). So it was done; but just as Moses had foreseen, the connections between the parts of Israel separated by the Jordan Valley became attenuated.

David at Mahanaim

Enthroned at Rabbath Ammon where the Jabbok rises, Nahash, king of Ammon, pressed his power as far west as the Jordan Valley. There he laid siege to Jabesh-gilead on its east side. The inhabitants of the city sought to make terms with him. He agreed—setting, however, a savage stipulation: "And Nahash the Ammonite said unto them, On this condition will I make . . . [a covenant] with you, namely, that all your right eyes be gouged out, bringing disgrace thus upon all Israel. And the elders of Jabesh [-gilead] said unto him, Give us seven days' respite, that we may send messengers unto all the borders of Israel; and then, if there be none to save us, we shall surrender ourselves to you" (I Samuel 11:2, 3). Nahash agreed, apparently convinced that help would not be forthcoming. What fun it would be to sit and watch his quarry squirm for seven days before completing his cruelty on them! He had reckoned without his host. Saul, not yet king, but merely a rugged peasant chieftain who could be seen in the evening "coming from the field behind the oxen" (I Samuel 11:5), was roused to wrath when he heard the words of the messengers of Jabesh. Having assembled the yeomen of Israel, he made a forced night march, descended into the valley, crossed the Jordan and attacked the unsuspecting Ammonites at dawn, smiting them from early morning "until the heat of the day: and it came to pass, that those who survived were scattered, with no two of them being left together" (I Samuel 11:11). The men of Jabesh-gilead long bore this kindness in mind, and the day would come when they would requite Saul with good for the salvation he had brought them.

In the course of time Hanun, the son of Nahash, succeeded to his father's throne, and David was well-disposed to him. Nahash had perhaps once done a favor for David, or perhaps they had drawn close to each other in their common hostility to Saul. Be that as it may, when Nahash died, David sent a deputation to Hanun with a message of condolence. But like father, like son! The churlish youth, accepting ill advice, became convinced that David had sent his servants merely to spy out Rabbath Ammon and make plans for its capture. "So Hanun took David's servants and shaved off half of the beard of each of them, and cut off their garments in the middle, at their buttocks, and sent them away. When it was told to David, he sent to meet them; for the men were greatly ashamed. And the king said, Tarry at Jericho until your beards be grown, and then return" (II Samuel 10:4, 5).

This was an insult that could not be lightly endured. The Ammonites and their Syrian allies were engaged in battle and defeated. Not satisfied to let well enough alone, the Syrians called up new forces and re-formed their ranks for attack. This time David, taking personal command, "gathered all Israel together, and crossed over the Jordan" (II Samuel 10:17) and inflicted such punishment upon them that "the Syrians feared to help the Bene-Ammon any more" (II Samuel 10:19). Rabbath Ammon was captured and looted. Ammon, Moab and Edom were then successively subjected to David's dominion.

The Jordan and the Jabbok were to figure frequently in David's life. Ishbaal, also called Ishbosheth, the sole surviving son of Saul, mounted after his father's death a shaky throne in Mahanaim, on the north bank of the Jabbok in East Jordan. His life would have been forfeit to David, the friend of his brother Jonathan, had he not fled there in good time. David, contending for the throne of Saul, had himself crowned king at Hebron, and after Ishbaal's death ultimately ruled supreme in Jerusalem. The violence he countenanced or pretended piously not to condone was, however, to pursue him to the end of his days. He was to be cursed to his face as a "man of blood and a base fellow" (II Samuel 16:7). In the evening of his career, he was to be compelled to forsake the comfort of his palace in Jerusalem and flee for his life from his own son Absalom, who in unfilial rebellion had been, like his father before him, crowned king in rowdy Hebron, a center of malcontents.

In my mind's eye I can see the aged sheikh David, seated on his donkey, departing to the fare of flight and danger which had been his daily bread in his younger days. I can see him and his faithful companions fording the Jordan, skirts tucked up to avoid the water, then making brief camp on the other side. I can see them climbing a steep path leading up a narrow canyon, through which runs a clear, strong stream. Is this not the River Jabbok? And is this not the path leading to that very Mahanaim to which Ishbosheth, the crippled son of Saul, once fled from David when David seized the crown in Hebron in usurpation of royal rights? What thoughts weigh down the weary shoulders of this refugee? No prophet Nathan is necessary this time to accuse him of having stolen the poor man's only ewe lamb. The rushing stream, the stabbing thorns, the frowning hills shout insistently, "The sin is thine, O David, and vengeance is the Lord's!" What punishment portended? How must he expiate his crimes? David's memories and his forebodings piled in on top of him like dark storm clouds.

But there at last was Mahanaim, the dwellings of friends and promise of rest and food. And what a heartwarming welcome he and his companions received: "And it came to pass, when David came to Mahanaim, that Shobi the [friendly] son of Nahash from Ammonite Rabbah, . . . and Machir, . . . and Barzillai . . . [each contributing from his family's store], brought beds and basins and pottery vessels and wheat and barley and flour, . . . and honey and butter and sheep and cheese of the herd for David and his people to eat; for they said, The people are weary and hungry and thirsty in the wilderness" (II Samuel 17:27–29).

I myself have often received similar food when living with Arabs in their tents. They have frequently served me *dibs* and *zibdeh* and *jibneh* and *dhabiheh*, with piles of round thin flaps of their lovely unleavened bread: *dibs*, something like honey, usually made of dates; *zibdeh*, butter of sheep or goat or kine; *jibneh*, cheese of various kinds; *dhabiheh*, a sheep or goat, slaughtered on the guest's arrival, cooked and served up on a great platter, filled with rice or burghul, roasted grains of wheat. And on numerous occasions my thirst has been quenched with *lebn*, thin sour cream, or *sheninah*, buttermilk! A beaker full of it is heaven to a thirsty man.

David's darkest hour was yet to come. Absalom's army, crossing the Jordan in hot pursuit of the faithful forces of David, was finally allowed to join battle with them at a place of the latter's choosing, and it was cut to pieces. Absalom had to flee for his life among the rough hills and thick woods of Gilead, in the region known today as the Jebel Ajlun. There towers the ruin of the great medieval castle of Qalat er-Rabad, a landmark from afar overlooking the beginnings of the Wadi Kufrinji. The woods of oak and pine are still thick, and one can still ride for hours under their shade. My clothes have been torn and my face whipped by their branches as I have pushed through them on many occasions.

"And Absalom was riding upon his mule, and the mule went under the thick boughs of a great oak, and his hair caught fast in the branches of

97

the oak; and he was left dangling between heaven and earth, while the mule he had been riding continued on" (II Samuel 18:9). In this position he was found, and the darts that David's general, Joab, thrust through the heart of the hapless youth were in effect to pierce also the heart of his father when the news was conveyed to him. What had he further to hope for, as he sat between the gates of Mahanaim hugging his grief to his bosom? Aged, bereft of a dearly beloved if wayward son, whose violence had been after the manner of his own father—had it not been better if the son had lived and David through death had found expiation and peace? "O my son Absalom, my son, my son Absalom! Would I had died instead of you, O Absalom, my son, my son!" (II Samuel 18:33). But as surely as the Jabbok by which he raised his lament flowed into the Jordan, and the Jordan into the Sea of Death, so inevitable, David brooded, had been the consequences of his living, the death of his hope. "O Absalom, my son, my son!"

The Decapolis city of Gerasa

About 10 miles to the east-northeast of Mahanaim, where David bemoaned the death of his errant son, located in a rich valley of the hill country veined by more-or-less north–south branches of the eastern beginnings of the River Jabbok (Wadi Zerqa), are the glorious remains of the great Hellenistic-Roman and Byzantine city of Gerasa (modern Jerash). In the beginning, Gerasa was one of the outstanding members of the loose confederation of Decapolis cities to which, among others, Philadelphia (Amman), Pella, Gadara and Abila belonged in Transjordan and Scythopolis (Beisan) in Palestine. The magnificent structures erected in Gerasa in the Byzantine period, including some of the finest churches of early Christendom, were not able to obscure the magnificence of the earlier Hellenistic-Roman city, which Nabataean traders and caravans, among others, frequently visited and where fragments of Nabataean pottery and remains of a Nabataean sanctuary have been found. There too was unearthed the mosaic floor of a Byzantine synagogue on which scenes of the Biblical Flood story are depicted.

The existing ruins of Gerasa dramatically help recreate for the modern visitor the appearance of Herodian Caesarea Philippi, Tiberias and Jericho in the Jordan Valley as well as the contemporary Hellenistic-Roman Scythopolis and other cities of the same general period such as Gadara, overlooking the Sea of Galilee, Sebastieh (former Shechem and modern Nablus) in the center of the hill country of Israelite Samaria and Caesarea Maritima on the Mediterranean coast. When Jesus visited Caesarea Philippi at the Paneas source of the Jordan, he saw pagan temples similar to the Temple of Artemis in Gerasa with its proudly upthrusting Corinthian columns and capitals or its Temple of Zeus overlooking the impressive Forum and the main paved thoroughfare. Alongside it at Gerasa were a hippodrome, theaters, a vaulted bathhouse and a circular market place the stalls of which were laden with the goods of the Orient and Occident.

The fertile hill country of North Gilead, in the southern part of which Gerasa is located, was occupied by sedentary agricultural civilizations from earliest historical times. This is true also of the rest of Transjordan, once forested but with still-excellent agricultural and grazing uplands. Both to the east and west of the Wadi Jerash, for example, are many ancient sites, some of which belong to periods long before the Hellenistic-Byzantine times of Gerasa. These periods of occupation include Iron Age I and II (between the thirteenth and sixth centuries B.C.), in which the Ammonites, Amorites and others were locally resident; the Middle Bronze I period of the time of Abraham (twenty-first to nineteenth centuries B.C.) and the Chalcolithic and Early Bronze periods (fourth millennium to the first part of the third millennium B.C.). We have even found sites in the Jordan Valley proper belonging, as evidenced by surface finds, to the Pottery Neolithic period, which can be dated to the fifth millennium B.C.

The most important site along the small Wadi Jerash, which cuts its way southward to meet the main east–west course of the Wadi Zerqa (River Jabbok), is Gerasa of the Decapolis. Situated in the center of good agricultural lands, containing many strong and perennial springs, it was long a surprise not that Gerasa grew to its great size and importance in Hellenistic-Roman-Byzantine times but that apparently it had been established on virgin soil, its foundations disturbing no ancient remains of earlier settlements. That seemed all the more strange because of the strong perennial spring, now called Ain Qeirawan, emerging at the base of the hills on the east side of Gerasa. The builders of Roman Gerasa enclosed the spring of Ain Qeirawan in a fine masonry basin. Its waters are still drawn by the Circassian and Arab inhabitants of modern Jerash, which nestles among the eastern ruins of Gerasa, on the east side of the small Wadi Jerash. The apparent absence of an ancient settlement despite the presence of a good spring was contrary to all previous experience.

At the disposal of the inhabitants of ancient and modern Gerasa have long been the perennial waters of the Wadi Jerash, flowing southward through the center of the town to empty ultimately—to the extent they have not been used up for irrigation purposes—into the Wadi Zerqa. In view of this sturdy supply of water, it seems reasonable to believe that the entire Jerash region—particularly the rich valley between Jerash proper and the powerful springs of Birketein and Ain Shewahid near and at the valley's north end—and the surrounding hillsides were intensively cultivated in the period of Abraham and perhaps back to the fourth millennium B.C. By the same token, one would have expected to find another early-Bronze Age site near Birketein, the strong spring just mentioned, which is found less than a mile to the north of the North Gate of Jerash. In Roman times a colonnade stood around the pool, and close by was a small theater known as the Festival Theater. Thus far, however, such an early site has not been found either at the spring of Birketein or of Ain Shewahid, although we are confident that traces of it will be discovered someday. In the vicinity of Remeimin, for instance, not very far from Jerash on the south side of the Wadi Zerqa, we found a whole cluster of early Bronze Age sites within a short distance of each other in the vicinity of several powerful springs.

The general rule that an ancient site or series of ancient sites should exist in the vicinity of a strong spring of sweet water proved to be correct some years ago, when after many seasons of vain searching, we finally came across an Abrahamic-and-earlier fortified hilltop settlement immediately overlooking the east side of Gerasa and the nearby spring of Ain Qeirawan. The site was so inconspicuous and seemed so completely natural that somehow it had escaped being examined by archaeologists. In the company of Walter Clay Lowdermilk, then Chief of Research of the Soil Conservation Service of the United States Department of Agriculture, and Reginald Head, then of the Transjordan Department of Lands and Forests, we were examining the top of the outer east wall of Roman Gerasa. I had taken them there particularly to show Dr. Lowdermilk how the soil, for centuries washed down by the rains from the slopes of the hill east and immediately above the wall, had mounted in many places to the top of the outer face of the wall and in places even spilled over it to pile up against its inner base.

The ancient terraces safeguarding the slopes of the hill from erosion had for the most part been neglected for centuries. Wherever in the neighborhood, however, the terraces by chance remained intact or had been kept in good repair, the soil has been kept in place; elsewhere winter and spring rains have swept it away and exposed bare and sterile rock.

While walking on the top of the northeast corner of this Gerasa outer east wall and noting the ravages of neglect, we spotted some fragments of pottery that had been washed down with the soil from the slope above. Most of them were Roman or Byzantine, but among them was one that clearly belonged to the Middle Bronze I period of the Age of Abraham. While that sherd was startling, a single sherd does not in itself testify to the existence of an entire period of settlement any more than a single swallow makes a summer. It induced us, however, to look for other fragments of pottery on the slope above. Following the trail of other sherds of the same early period and of the Early Bronze Age and the latter part of the still-earlier Chalcolithic period, we came to the summit of a low flat-top hill overlooking Gerasa and its spring. Further examination showed that the entire hilltop had been surrounded originally by a strong, outer fortification wall, considerable traces of which remained, even though worn down or destroyed to the surface level. This was in keeping with a common though not unvarying practice during the early Bronze Age (and later periods) to fortify great hilltops with massive outer walls and cultivate the slopes and valleys below them, as well as much of the enclosed hilltop itself.

The presence of a spring immediately below the hill, its strategic location and the existence of fertile soil on its slopes and in neighboring fields made it almost inevitable for Gerasa to have been occupied at a very early age. During its various periods of occupation, its inhabitants undoubtedly engaged in agriculture, viticulture and animal husbandry. Sometime early in the nineteenth century B.C. a great catastrophe occurred, resulting probably from a devastating war, that brought the entire Middle Bronze I civilization of the Age of Abraham, extending from Syria to the borders of Egypt, to an absolute end. The tragic destruction of the settlements of this period is mirrored, as already described, in the story of the war of the "kings of the east" against the kings of the cities along the Dead Sea (Genesis 14).

For some six centuries thereafter, Bedouins roamed the land, pitching their tents wherever it pleased them. With the exception of perhaps several fortified cities built in Middle Bronze II between the nineteenth and sixteenth centuries B.C., there were no fortresses or permanent settlements or strong governmental forces to stay the wanderings of the Bedouins and push them back to the deserts whence they came. Then, at the end of the fourteenth, early in the thirteenth century B.C. a new period of sedentary agricultural civilization ensued, belonging to the Edomites, Moabites, Ammonites and Amorites. They preceded the advent of the Israelites by several generations, and were strong enough to banish the Bedouins once again to the desert wilderness and prevent fairly effectively their forays into areas brought under cultivation. Although obscured in the haze of ancient history, these peoples were fully as real as the Israelites.

The Israelites and Judaeans had gifted writers who chronicled, sometimes in much detail and other times merely in outline, the history of their people as illustrative material for the theological purposes of the Bible. Fate or Providence has kept both the people of Israel and the Book alive. The historians among the contemporaries of the Israelites on the east side of the Jordan were probably equally gifted in composing narrative accounts of their peoples' adventures, and must also have kept historical records similar to the "Book of the Wars of the Lord" and other source books referred to in the Bible. They may or may not have had the theologians like those of Israel and Judah who culled materials from various archives to compile in fixed form for general edification their religious beliefs and practices and principles. Unfortunately, documents of this nature, which must have existed among these ancient Iron Age kingdoms of Transjordan, have not been handed down to us, any more than has the "Book of Yashar" referred to in the Bible. But the fact that we do not possess them or that they have not yet been found can hardly be interpreted to mean that they did not once exist. The evidence of the Moabite stone, describing in beautifully incised characters (indistinguishable from contemporaneous Hebrew ones) how Mesha, king of Moab, regained the independence of his country from Ahab, king of Israel, at or near the end of the latter's reign in 852 B.C., demonstrates the high literary capabilities of the Moabites.

Even if extensive excavations were undertaken at many sites in Edom, Moab, Ammon or Gilead, there is little hope that writings on parchment, leather or other perishable materials will have escaped the ravages of time. Inscriptions on stone or pottery can, however, withstand moisture and chemical action and indeed have already been found at various places in

Transjordan. Sometimes even ink writing on such materials may through accident escape destruction. As a matter of fact, more important documents of durable materials have already been found accidentally on the surface in Transjordan than have been discovered in excavations dealing with the early history of Palestine and Transjordan in the Iron Age. One thinks primarily, of course, of the famous Moabite stele just mentioned, but also of the famous stele found at Baluah near the Wadi Mojib, assigned to the twelfth century B.C., whose worn lines of inscription can unfortunately no longer be read. Happily, under proper climatic conditions and circumstances, millennia-old writings on perishable materials such as parchment, leather and copper have survived, as evidenced by the Dead Sea Scrolls and their like.

Let it not be thought, therefore, that so far as any of the trappings of culture are concerned, the Edomites or Moabites or any of their contemporaries in Transjordan were backward, or that they possessed a material civilization less advanced than that which flourished on the west side of the Jordan. In most respects, all these groups developed similar cultures and were of the same or closely related ethnic stock. They made much the same kind of pottery, used the same kinds of tools and weapons and ornaments, built the same kinds of houses and fortresses, wore the same kind of clothes, spoke and wrote essentially the same western Semitic language, and worshiped, so far as the general masses of people were concerned, the same fertility gods. The different fates of these peoples cannot be explained, except perhaps through the concept of God and the covenant with Him that ultimately became supremely important to the people of Israel and Judah and their physical and spiritual descendants.

Gaps in sedentary settlement

The Semites who took possession of Transjordan at the end of the fourteenth or the beginning of the thirteenth century B.C. probably absorbed and partly drove out the Bedouins who since about 1900 B.C. had been the masters of the land. The new occupants, taking up agricultural pursuits, soon broke up into smaller, more natural groupings. The new divisions probably originally reflected separate families or tribes, their separateness overcoming their general relatedness. Today, for instance, we find the Beni

Sakhar tribe in control of large areas in northern Transjordan, and the Howeitat tribe in control of much of southern Transjordan, separated by geographic rather than ethnic factors.

Fully as important, however, for the partition of Transjordan into the kingdoms of Edom, Moab, Ammon and the two Amorite kingdoms of Gilead were the natural land divisions of the country. The "other" or east side of the Jordan is bounded on the west by the Wadi Arabah, the Dead Sea and the Jordan River Valley. On the east and south it is bounded by the desert. The kingdoms within this area were marked off in the main from each other, as we have seen, by the wide and deep natural boundaries of the Wadi Hesa (the River Zered), the Wadi Mojib (the River Arnon), the Wadi Zerqa (the River Jabbok) and the Wadi Yarmuk, counting from south to north.

Within these limits, the kingdoms of the Edomites, Moabites, Ammonites and Amorites in East Jordan developed swiftly during the Iron Age. The main period of their development extended between the thirteenth and the eighth centuries B.C., after which a period of deterioration set in, culminating in complete destruction in the sixth century B.C. The excavations, particularly at Dhiban (Dibon), conducted by F. V. Winnett and A. D. Tushingham, revealed a gap in the history of sedentary occupation extending from approximately 1850 to 1300 B.C. This break in the story of agricultural civilization, ascertained through excavations in depth, confirmed thus the conclusions arrived at from our archaeological surface explorations of Transjordan, particularly from the River Jabbok southward.

The Iron Age kingdoms of Transjordan were highly advanced and strongly organized. The land was dotted with well-built stone villages and towns. The borders of their kingdoms, which can now be accurately fixed, were fortified by strong fortresses, usually built on eminences and commanding a view of each other. Their agriculture was intensive, their pottery well made, their commerce sensibly ordered, their literature in all probability of no mean quality, if one may draw inferences from the inscription of Mesha or the early narrative framework of the later dramatic poem known as the Book of Job. The wealth of these kingdoms, even under Assyrian domination, may be judged from the tribute paid to Esarhaddon. Edom paid 12 manas of silver in comparison with 10 manas of silver paid by Judah; Ammon paid 2 manas of gold; Moab paid 1 mana of gold. The greatness of these kingdoms was, in a word, very real, however scant the literary remains of their existence.

Early in the sixth century B.C., the Iron Age civilizations on both sides of the Jordan were destroyed, including of course such towns as Mahanaim on the Jabbok, associated with Ishbosheth and David's flight from Absalom, and the city of the same period that must have existed somewhere in the precincts of Gerasa. There followed then, especially in Transjordan from South Gilead southward, the Wadi Arabah and the Negev, another break in the history of civilized sedentary settlement that lasted for approximately three centuries and more. Once again the Bedouins tented at will in the lands of the Sown, which comparatively speaking were always richer, better watered and infinitely more desirable than the wastes of the Desert. The vacuum caused by the absence of organized governmental power that made possible their coming was removed at the beginning of the Hellenistic-Roman and Nabataean periods, when cities like Gerasa and Petra were established and temples such as that of Nabataean Khirbet Tannur came into being.

The pronounced breaks in the history of sedentary settlement in much of Transjordan, in the Wadi Arabah and the Negev resulted generally speaking in the absence of *tulul,* artificial city-hills. These were formed normally, as we have seen, by the practically unbroken succession during many centuries of one city being built on top of the ruins of the preceding one. In Palestine proper and in North Gilead in the northernmost part of Transjordan, such layered mounds of history are to be found in large numbers. They dot the length of the Jordan Valley. The dull grayishness of their appearance, distinguishing them from the brownish soil of the valley above which they are somewhat elevated, make them easily recognizable both from the ground and from the air.

Jephthah's daughter

What sights an ancient land sees during the centuries, and what stories its stones could tell! Listen! Whence came these unbridled lamentations that tear the silence from the sides of the Jabbok canyon? What searing sadness has burned laughter from women's lips and made them shriek endlessly, with a yielding more unrestrained to sorrow than to a passionate embrace? And then, suddenly, singing! Sweet singing, swelling fiercely, subsiding sadly, followed by clamorous silence. What frightful fate has befallen a fellow mortal? Bursting through the thicket into an open meadow on top of a high hill, which from time immemorial had been devoted to divinity, we behold a group of maidens gathered around—yes, now we know—gathered around the daughter of Jephthah! The dread tale has been bruited about. Quickly, now, back into the woods before being observed! And away, hasten away, and leave them to weep out their sorrow in solitude! Never shall we forget the dark-haired, sun-kissed, slim virgin, robed in deathless white, standing frozen, silent, in the midst of her company!

Below, far below, ran the waters of the Jabbok to the Jordan. Because of her father's war for the security of the Jabbok and the safety of Israel was Jephthah's daughter to die? What grievous burden to lay on soft shoulders that no lover's hand had yet caressed, nor now would ever touch! This had happened before the prophet said, "Every one shall die for his own iniquity; every man who eats sour grapes, his teeth shall be set on edge" (Jeremiah 31:30; compare Ezekiel 18:2). In vain had Jephthah attempted to dissuade the king of Ammon from seizing territory not his on the basis of trumped-up historical allegations. Insistently had he urged him to remember that the lands he now demanded had been held by Israel for three hundred years without its claim ever being questioned. Long ago, in fair fight with Sihon, king of the Amorites, who had denied Israel access through his territory to the Jordan, Israel had come into possession of "all the territory of the Amorites, from the Arnon unto the Jabbok, and from the wilderness even unto the Jordan" (Judges 11:22). But when have men of violence listened to judicious counsel? "But the king of the Bene-Ammon disregarded the message that Jephthah sent him" (Judges 11:28). So Jephthah made ready for war.

Fierce soul of simple sentiment, Jephthah made a vow that if he emerged victorious from the impending battle he would give as a gift to God the first thing he saw when he returned home, thinking no doubt of one of his fat sheep or heavy bulls of Bashan. Assured thus in his heart of divine intervention in his behalf because of his irrevocable vow, "Jephthah advanced against the Bene-Ammon to fight against them. . . . And he smote them, . . . so that the Bene-Ammon were subdued before the Bene-Israel" (Judges 11:32, 33). His duty done, Jephthah hastened to his home at Mizpah in Gilead. Now, he thought, rubbing his hands in pleasurable anticipation as he neared his dwelling, which of his animals would be the first to cross his path to be served as a sacrifice to his success? And then the castle of his joy collapsed and his heart was crushed within him. Running to meet the grizzled warrior was his carefree, dearly beloved daughter, about whom his own life revolved. The news of his coming had outsped him. Panting for sight of him, his only child had run like a gazelle to be the first of his family to reach him. Now indeed he was undone by Ammon and by his own primitive faith, from which he knew no retreat.

"And Jephthah came to Mizpah unto his house; and behold, his daughter came out to meet him with timbrels and with dances. She was his only child; besides her he had neither son nor daughter. And it came to pass, when he saw her, he rent his clothes, and said, Alas, my daughter! you have brought me very low, and have become one of those that trouble me; for I have opened my mouth unto the Lord and I cannot break my word" (Judges 11:34, 35). No cry of consternation from the warrior-daughter! No piteous plea for retraction of the perverse promise! "And she said unto him, My father, if you have made a commitment to the Lord, so then you must fulfill your undertaking, inasmuch as the Lord has taken vengeance for you on your enemies, even on the Bene-Ammon. And she said unto her father, Let this thing be done for me: grant me two months grace, that I may depart and spend some time by the mountains and bewail my virginity, I and my companions. And he said, Go. . . . And it came to pass at the end of two months, that she returned to her father, who did with her according to the vow he had made: and she had known no man. And it became a custom in Israel, that the daughters of Israel went four days every year to memorialize the daughter of Jephthah the Gileadite" (Judges 11:36–40).

Where was her retreat in the mountains? On a windswept height overlooking the steep descent to the River Jabbok is a small, tumbledown stone structure standing close to a gnarled oak tree. In the crevices of the building, and hanging from the branches of the tree, are pitiful little rags and bits of string, placed there by poor pilgrims in token of fervent vows. Such are their offerings to the god of nature, long considered resident on this commanding hilltop. It matters not that the worshipers now are superficially Moslems, who profess adherence to one God, Allah, and who incline according to the instructions of his prophet Mohammed. The patrons of this sanctuary are essentially pagans, by whatever name they may be known. With humility and wonder in their hearts, they beat difficult ways to the shrine of an ancient god whose mode of worship is dim in their memories but whose hold is strong on their souls. I like to think that it was to this high place, once green with woods, overlooking the Jabbok River from the south, that the daughter of Jephthah and her companions retired, and the maidens of Israel long thereafter repaired to wail over her untimely death.

At this juncture in his life, how ill-advised of the men of Ephraim to offer affront to Jephthah! They dared raise angry accusation against him because, forsooth, he had fought the Ammonites without them. Raucous voices shrilled vehement denunciation, all the more vicious because of underlying falsehood. In truth he had called them to help, but receiving no reply had acted independently while there was yet time. Was this the hero's reward? Was boundless insult to be heaped now upon his fathomless sorrow? His sacrifice had, after all, saved them too! In this hour of his heaviness of heart they had actually taken up arms against him. They were even threatening to burn down his house, the house in which Jephthah's daughter had once sat and sung! To his undying credit be it said that Jephthah remonstrated with these ingrates of Ephraim who had become brave when victory was won. Unable to dissuade them, he attacked their camp at Zaphon on the east side of the Jordan Valley, to which they had come from their western hills. So thoroughly were they defeated that no refuge was left even for straggling fugitives. The few who sought in disguise to recross the Jordan betrayed themselves by their peculiar accent to Jephthah's guards stationed at its fords.

The Bible has graphically recorded this entire incident: "And the men of Ephraim were gathered together and crossed over to Zaphon and said to Jephthah, How did it happen that you crossed over to fight against the Bene-Ammon without calling us to go with you? We will burn your house with fire. And Jephthah said unto them, I and my people were in grievous strife with the Bene-Ammon. When I called you, you made no move to deliver me from them. And when I saw that you had no intention of helping, I took my life in my hand, and crossed over against the Bene-Ammon, and the Lord delivered them into my hand: why then have you come up to me this day to fight against me? Then Jephthah gathered together all the men of Gilead, and . . . smote Ephraim, . . . and . . . took the fords of the Jordan against the Ephraimites. And it was so, that when any of the fugitives of Ephraim said, Let me go over, the men of Gilead said unto him, . . . Say now Shibboleth; and he said Sibboleth; for he could not pronounce it right; in such an instance they took hold of him and slew him at the fords of the Jordan" (Judges 12:1–6).

Where was Zaphon?

Where was Zaphon, the scene of the Ephraimite debacle and of other important happenings mentioned in the Bible? Among the many ancient sites whose ruins remain in the Jordan Valley, which is to be identified with Zaphon? The modern names of these Jordan Valley places give no hint of their original designations. Only through their present prefixes of tell and khirbeh (ruin) do they vaguely reveal the fact of former habitation. These forgotten mounds of foundations of ancient settlements were once composed of successive groups of houses vibrant with human sounds. Village elders deliberated in the gateways; the hubbub of traffic filled the air. Now merely sad symbols of snuffed-out life, the uncultivable ruins are sought out by tent-dwellers in the Jordan Valley as burial grounds for their dead or, being raised above the moist valley floor, are used to house dry grainpits, where surplus wheat and barley are cannily stored.

Even vague references, however, give important clues. Fragments of pottery, more indestructible than stone, are eloquent of the period of their construction and the manner of the civilization in which the pottery was produced. Contours of the landscape, sources of water and routes of travel also help. In such wise Zaphon has been identified with Tell Qos.

Tell Qos in the Jordan Valley is on a high, flat-top, completely isolated hill on the north side of the River Rajeb, near its outlet from the eastern hills. It commands a splendid view over much of the valley and over the further course of the Wadi Rajeb westward toward its junction with the Jordan. It is an obvious strategic center on an important crossroads, one branch of which leads up into the hills of Gilead, where Mizpah, the home of Jephthah, lay. The masters of Tell Qos were in a position to give or withhold permission to use the waters of the Rajeb stream, and held thus the welfare of the farmers of the district in their hands, for agriculture was possible only through irrigation. The Rajeb is north of the River Jabbok and, according to the Bible, Zaphon is the first important district center on the east side of the valley, north of Succoth (located near the entrance of the Jabbok into the Jordan Valley). Tell Qos is the only site which can be equated with Zaphon.

The early age of Zaphon is indicated by its name, which shows that it was a sanctuary of Baal-zaphon, long worshiped in the land before being displaced by devotion to invisible Jahweh. When I climbed to the top of

Tell Qos one day to map its ruins and collect the fragments of pottery strewn on its surface, recapitulating its more than 3000 years of occupation, I saw a harmless madman sitting there, a majnun, one of those touched by the Djin, who evoke a sense of awe among their more normal fellows. I tried to talk to him, but could not tear him from his introspection. I wondered what were his connections with the past. What visions of yesteryear could he conjure up? What shades or spirits of forgotten eras and events could he commune with?

The loud-mouthed Ephraimites had finally been taught a lesson they should long previously have learned. On an earlier occasion, Gideon of Abiezer had had to contend with them, because, like Jephthah, without waiting for their aid, he had delivered Israel from Midianite oppression. Then too the men of Ephraim had upbraided their savior for the victory he had won for them. "And the men of Ephraim said to him, We take umbrage that you failed to summon us when you went to fight with Midian. And they chided him sharply. And he said unto them, What have I now done in comparison with you? Is not the gleaning of the grapes of Ephraim better than the vintage of Abiezer? . . . Then their anger was abated against him" (Judges 8:1–3).

Gideon, Jacob and Esau

The Midianites and other Bedouins were wont at harvest time to make rapid raids across the Jordan, carry away the crops of Israel from the threshing floors and drive off whatever livestock they could lay their hands on. The struggle between the Desert and the Sown is continuous. Hungry nomads have ever pressed into plowed lands, content to take by swift violence what others have gained by hard toil. When Gideon was summoned to head off the raiders, he himself "was beating out wheat in the winepress, to hide it from the Midianites" (Judges 6:11). Gideon and his band dispersed the Bedouins, who retreated eastward across the Jordan. Inflicting severe punishment upon them, they pursued them hotly into and beyond the hills of Gilead, until finally the raiders lost themselves in the reaches of the desert.

On the way through the Jordan Valley and up the difficult path zigzagging to the top of the Jabbok canyon, Gideon and his troops, faint from hunger, had been badly received by the men of Succoth and Penuel. He had promised himself and them to repay their conduct in kind once the chase was over. "When Gideon . . . returned from the battle, . . . he caught hold of a lad from Succoth, and pressed him to write down the names of seventy-seven of the princes and elders of Succoth" (Judges 8:13, 14). (The incident provides eloquent evidence of the high degree of literacy prevailing among the general population.) In his hour of need the men of Succoth had refused him help, so now Gideon "took the elders of the city, and thorns of the wilderness and briars, and with them he taught the men of Succoth. And he also broke down the tower of Penuel, and slew the men of the city" (Judges 8:16, 17).

Stranger scenes than these had been enacted still earlier on the banks of the Jabbok as it flowed by the sites of Penuel and Succoth on its way to the Jordan. Had not one of the patriarchs seen God face to face at Penuel? Jacob was returning from his long sojourn in Mesopotamia, where he had acquired a large family and much wealth in service with his father-in-law Laban. He had fled to that far-off land originally to escape the wrath of his brother Esau, whose rights as firstborn he had bought for a mess of pottage and whose blessing as firstborn he had obtained from their blind father by trickery. Twenty years had elapsed, and now Jacob's face turned homeward. The nearer he came, the sharper the conflict in his soul. He hesitated to cross the Jabbok. Inner torment gave him no peace. The years had not laid to rest his fear of Esau's anger. The voice of his conscience had no more been silenced than the flow of the Jabbok had been stopped. He had wronged his father; he had robbed his brother. Would punishment finally catch up with him? Would he ever again be able to cross the Jordan and live the rest of his life on his native heath?

"And he rose up that night, and took his two wives and . . . his eleven children, and passed over the ford of the Jabbok. And he took them, and sent them over the stream, and all that which he had. And Jacob was left alone; and there wrestled a man with him until the breaking of the day. And when he saw that he could not prevail against him [Jacob], he touched the hollow of his thigh; and Jacob's thigh was strained as he wrestled with him. And he said, Let me go, because day is breaking. And he replied, I will not let you go, unless you bless me. Whereupon he said unto him, What is your name? And he said, Jacob. And he said, Your name shall be no more called Jacob, but Israel, meaning he who strives with God: for you have striven with God and with men, and have prevailed.... And he blessed him there. And Jacob called the name of the place Penuel [the face of God]: saying, I have seen God face to face, and yet my life is preserved. And the sun rose upon him as he passed over Penuel, limping because of his thigh. Therefore the children of Israel eat not the sinew of the hip which is upon the hollow of the thigh, to this day: because he touched the hollow of Jacob's thigh" (Genesis 32:22–32).

I once slept overnight on top of Tell edh-Dhahab (the "Hill of Gold"), which is probably to be identified with Penuel. The canyon walls widen out considerably at this point, as the hills through which the Jabbok cuts its way begin to tumble down toward the Jordan Valley. The rushing little stream in the wadi-bed curves around the base of this hill on three sides, and in flood season cuts it off altogether from the mainland, as if to say, "This is a particularly important place, not to be associated with the mundane world." From the top of the hill there is a good view over the Jordan Valley and across it to the hills of Palestine. Some sense of sanctity still seems to be associated with this place. My Arab companions were most loath to have me sleep alone on the summit, and would on no condition accompany me there to spend the night. They made their camp at the foot of the hill, warning me that if I persisted in my intention to sleep on top of it, a spirit (the Djin) would seize me during the night, and that if indeed I did survive the ordeal I would wake up in the morning bereft of my senses. But here, I felt sure, Jacob wrestled during the night with his adversary, being left alone only at the break of dawn. And here I would sleep or sit out the night, the living past breathing its vivid tale into my ears. What would happen to me before I crossed the Jordan again? I slept. What are those sounds? The sighs of Jacob, the accents of Esau? Dawn had come! My Arabs had been shouting to me to come down, concerned for my safety.

Inwardly purified, Jacob made ready to meet his brother. His fears proved vain. Esau accepted his gifts and forgave the crime committed against him. "And Jacob lifted up his eyes, and looked, and, behold, Esau was coming, and with him four hundred men. ... And Esau ran to meet him, and embraced him, and fell on his neck, and kissed him: and they wept" (Genesis 33:1–4). Long they talked, neither at first quite convinced of the other's intentions, till at last, in complete reconciliation, they parted again, each going his own way. "So Esau returned that day on his way to

Seir. And Jacob journeyed to Succoth and built himself a house and made booths for his cattle: Therefore the name of the place is called Succoth (Booths)" (Genesis 33:16, 17).

What a magnificent site Succoth occupies near the entrance of the Jabbok into the Jordan Valley, where it is unquestionably to be identified with Tell Deir-alla. But more about that anon.

Dolmen-builders

Long before the Bible was composed, long even before writing was invented, civilized life was stirring in the Jordan Valley and in the hills and plains above it. Man made tools and weapons of flint, and built houses and tombs, called dolmens, of huge slabs of stone, that probably belong to the Pre-Pottery Neolithic period and were used and reused for millennia thereafter. A later and smaller type of dolmen may date to the first half of the fourth millennium B.C., in the Middle Chalcolithic period. These monuments raised by the dolmen-builders have made their memory endure for some eight thousand years or more, and they could, if not removed by man, easily last another ten millennia. Otherwise little is known of these ancient artisans, whose skill enabled them to quarry and move by hand great stone blocks which today would require heavy machinery to lift. One thing is certain: the architects of these structures were not primitive troglodytes who burrowed for shelter in caves or simple shepherds who dwelt only in tents. They were experienced craftsmen and builders trained in the skills of their day, which may have included advanced agriculture. It hardly seems possible that they lived so long ago. Their past can easily be reconstructed. Let us try.

Look! Is not that a group of them, standing on the slope of a hill above the east side of the Jordan Valley? There below, in the distance, is the line of the Jabbok converging with that of the Jordan. Several men are examining a vertical outcrop of limestone, studying its seams and its grain. "Yes, this will do," they seem to say. Wooden wedges are inserted, powerful arms wield heavy stone hammers, and soon a mighty slab is broken off, measuring perhaps 7 feet long, 5 feet wide, and 2 feet thick. In slow succession, three others of approximately similar size are prepared, and then two smaller ones. Meanwhile, another group of workmen has been building a circular platform of stone blocks, which rises in several narrowing stages to a flat top. The great slabs are now tipped and turned over again and again till they are brought to the base of the platform and then, on rollers, pushed and pulled up a dirt incline to its top. These people understand the principles of leverage! Sweat pours freely from their faces, and the strain makes the veins on their arms and foreheads stand out. But still it is careful skill rather than brute force that makes it possible to move these megaliths. One of the stones is laid flat, two others are set up lengthwise on their narrow sides, three feet apart, then another great stone laid over them as a roof. Now the tomb is ready for its occupant! The funeral procession approaches and the body is inserted, with a few flint tools and some food for the long journey in the afterlife. Then the ends are sealed with smaller slabs. Now everyone joins in the work, and a mound of dirt is heaped over the massive cairn. Farewell, dear departed!

Who among the mourners could know that long, very long after your bones have disintegrated into dust, your gravestones will still be standing? But your sleep will not remain undisturbed for long. Human moles will burrow into your bed to seize the few possessions buried with you. Several thousand years later, your kind will have been wiped off the face of the earth or merged with newcomers, and other men of different groups will have lain, each in his turn and period, in your place. The process will often be repeated. Down through the ages, your last dwelling will house new corpses from passing populations. The day will come when Roman and Byzantine pottery will be found on the dolmen's floor.

At the edge of the Jordan Valley, on the hills and plateau above it and on the slopes in between lie these dolmens by the hundreds and thousands, littering the entire length of Transjordan. Dolmen fields stretch north into Syria, west into Palestine. Their builders belonged to a people so numerous that many of them spilled over into marginal lands, where at least flocks could be maintained if crops could not be cultivated. They apparently worked separate farms and lived in long, narrow, thick-walled houses resembling the dolmens.

High in the hills of Transjordan, near the modern Arab village of Kefr Kifya, I stumbled across the remains of what I believe to be one of their massive houses. Its two long walls are still standing, made of rude flint blocks with small chunks of stone between. It measured 33 feet long, 25 feet wide, and was probably originally about 6 feet high. Each wall is about

7 feet thick. Over them at one time was a roof, made perhaps of wooden beams. Even if this should prove not to be one of their houses, can the thought be sensibly entertained that the men who built dolmen tombs, some of them two stories high or two chambers broad, or two chambers long with a pierced connecting partition, could not or would not have built homes for the living?

What catastrophe overcame these early inhabitants of the Jordan Valley and the neighboring lands? Perhaps they suffered the fate which was to be the common lot of all their successors. Living on the fringe of the desert and constantly exposed to the forays of the Bedouins, they were finally overwhelmed. The newcomers who took their places were transformed in time into tillers of the soil. And new nomads dispossessed them in turn. Horites and Amorites, Aramaeans and Israelites, Nabataeans and Arabs, Crusaders and Mongols invaded the land and remained to farm its fields. Each time hundreds or possibly thousands of natives were massacred and other thousands were driven away. Always, however, a large number remained, often to enslave their new masters partially or completely by giving them their gods and their blood, although not always their knowledge and attainments.

The only physical things that have remained permanent in the Jordan Valley are the flow of the Jordan and its tributaries and the comparative fertility of the soil on either side of it, conditioned as they are by the country's physical geography. Split in two by the fateful river and strait-jacketed between the Mediterranean Sea on the west and the desert on the east and south, this narrow strip of the Holy Land, "flowing with milk and honey," has been continuously coveted and frequently conquered by strangers.

"East ruin of the Mother of Hamad"

If one can imagine a spotlight moving across a darkened stage of history, illuminating past periods and places, let it now be considered to be lighting up the peninsulalike projection of the Jordan Valley caught between the junction of the Jabbok and Jordan rivers. The light now moves through the darkness to pick out a very large town. Square-built, flat-roofed, mud-brick houses become visible, with narrow lanes threading between them. There is a kiln, with rows of pots arranged in front of it, some already baked and ready for use. Look at that pottery, you connoisseurs! Are not these the types in use during most of the last five hundred years of the fourth millennium B.C. and belonging, in terms of scientific jargon, to the Late Chalcolithic and Early Bronze Ia periods? The spotlight has turned away! I should like to have seen more. Who lived in those houses, and where had they learned to make that pottery? What were the people like in appearance? Ah, now the light is back again! But what has happened in between? What sudden tornado visited this town, sweeping its houses into piles of debris and smashing its wares into thousands of pieces? Was the devastation wrought by raiders from the desert or other destructive invaders from afar, who wiped out in a flash the wealth that labor and love had built up in centuries of civilized existence?

I have walked over the ruins of this ancient site, whose former name we do not know. Today it is called Khirbet Umm Hamad Sherqi, the "East Ruin of the Mother of Hamad." Fragments of pottery can be picked up in great numbers on the surface of an area about a mile and a quarter long and a quarter of a mile wide. They are practically all that remain of a highly civilized center that must have been widely known in its time. In fact, without the sherds, it would be almost impossible to recognize the place as the location of an ancient city. More pottery was once used there than exists in the entire Jordan Valley today. Many of the present Arab inhabitants of the valley have reverted to the use of skins for containers. For them at least, the art of ceramics is completely lost.

A thousand years went by before a new town sprang up about a quarter of a mile west of the older site. After only a few hundred years of existence it suffered the same fate of complete destruction. It is the one now known as the "West Ruin of the Mother of Hamad" (Khirbet Umm Hamad Gharbi). It is marked today by an extensive low rise, covered with pottery so typical of the period between approximately the twenty-first and nineteenth centuries B.C. (Middle Bronze I) that it could be used as a classroom example of its kind. This area was apparently not again inhabited by sedentary agriculturists until the Israelite period, during the Early Iron Age (thirteenth to the sixth centuries B.C.). The two ruined sites are in the midst of fields now once again being irrigated and cultivated. The present fellahin, who live in tents, have already constructed mud-brick granaries and, I am confident, will soon build mud-brick villages to dwell in. The Jordan Valley is again becoming dotted with thriving villages and towns as of yore. And so scene succeeds scene upon the stage of history as the drama goes on.

The rise and fall of Khirbet Umm Hamad Sherqi and Gharbi illustrate a process that was to become heartbreakingly familiar in the history of settlement in the Jordan Valley. Out of the era of earliest antiquity appeared men striving blindly for better things. Small discoveries were chanced upon, experiences were passed on from father to son, an ever-increasing mass of knowledge was acquired. Civilization began, the land was tilled, commerce was engaged in, and towns developed. Stone tools and then pottery came into being, with styles changing in different periods. Then such men were replaced by others, sometimes less advanced and more rapacious. Ages of emptiness set in until pioneers again assembled to make new attempts on the same sites, or near them, because the natural factors left them no other choices. Thus a new civilization would be built up and perhaps still further gains were made, or perhaps it retrogressed. And after a while this new effort would be brought to nought by still another invader, as unthinking and unfeeling as some careless person who pulls up an iris which has somehow sunk its roots and found nourishment in the desert.

Junction with the Jordan

THEY CROSSED OVER ON DRY LAND

Continuing southward, the sides of the narrowing plain (Ghor) crumble down to the Jungle (Zor) of the Jordan, which merges with the broadened banks of the Jabbok as the two streams unite. This area, irrigated by the Jabbok's waters, blooms into fragrant fertility, made all the more pleasant by contrast with the gaunt bareness of the hillsides above it. Dominating the rich bottomland is a small mound whose modern name, Tell Damieh, reflects the Biblical name Adamah. Its history began some time before the advent of the Israelites. The sherds found there show the arrival and final disappearance of this people, and the coming and going of others after them down through the first centuries of the present era. The comparatively small tell, located on a natural rise, guards the track to a crossing of the Jordan, whose position is approximately marked by the remains of a Roman bridge and by the new one which has now taken its place. Some years ago, a decrepit rope ferry plied its angular way across the swift current. Events alone, however, have scarred a mark at this point which neither men nor time can easily efface.

The Israelites of the Exodus had passed through the desert, having survived its sands and vicissitudes. And then the longed-for day had come. Ahead of the people lay the Jordan, and across the Jordan lay the Promised Land! Priests, proudly burdened by the Ark of the Covenant and followed by the people, impatient to have done with this last obstacle to their final settlement, approached the flooded banks of the river, bordering the land of their sustaining dream. And just then, in that awful moment of uncertainty which marks the change from the rutted familiar to the uncertain now, an astounding miracle occurred. The Jordan was split in two! A river in itself was an almost unbelievable miracle to these invaders from thirsty lands. To the wonder of its existence was now added another wonder. As tradition has it, hardly had the feet of the priests touched the turbid flood when "the waters coming from upstream stood still, forming a single solid mass, reaching northward from Adamah, as far as the fortress of Zarethan. And the waters going downstream to the Sea of the Arabah, the Salt Sea, were wholly cut off. . . . Whereupon the priests that carried the ark of the covenant of the Lord stood firmly on dry ground in the midst of the Jordan; and all Israel passed over on dry land, until the entire people had crossed over the Jordan" (Joshua 3:16, 17).

Is this a legendary portrayal of an incident which can rationally be explained? In this uneasy area of earthquakes, it is known that landslides have at times blocked the normal channel of the Jordan, forcing it after a while to chart a new course or refashion a familiar path through the temporary obstacle. Did the Israelites chance upon just such an occasion, enabling them to cross the river dry-shod? Once before, according to the ancient account, during their escape from Egypt, they had passed between the sundered walls of water of the Red Sea. Be that as it may, the first contact of Israel with the Jordan had in it the elements of a miracle, and the river remained strangely entwined with their subsequent history. From the very first it had fascinated them. To the very last it influenced their fortune and fate.

COPPER FOUNDRIES OF HIRAM OF TYRE
The wall of water which, according to the Biblical description, stretched northward from Adamah to the Mezad or Fortress of Zarethan bounded

one of the richest sections of the east side of the Jordan Valley. One day in that area, during the time when Solomon was building the Temple to the Lord in Jerusalem, as I reconstruct the scene in my imagination, a knot of workers was gathered around an earthen mold in a small foundry. The men were silent. The air was still. Suddenly a sigh of relief escaped them, and a glint of satisfaction lighted up momentarily the eyes of their leader. He was Hiram of Tyre, Solomon's master coppersmith. The son of an intermarriage between an Israelite woman of the Naphtali tribe that lived in the area between Lake Huleh and the Sea of Galilee and a Phoenician coppersmith, Hiram had followed in his father's footsteps. The copper pillars of Jachin and Boaz, which were to be set up on the porch of the Temple, had been successfully poured in their earthen molds. Hiram had designed these pillars and had decorated them on the top with exquisite lily ornamentation. Now he could rest for a moment, relishing the satisfaction of work well done, before consigning it in his mind to the limbo of past accomplishment and tackling other tasks which stimulated anew his creative energies.

Work was executed under Hiram's command at many places in the Jordan Valley. It was his duty and professional delight to provide for the Temple in Jerusalem sacred vessels and ornaments of metal, as shapely in form and exquisite in detail as could be found anywhere in his Phoenician homeland and which would delight his mother's people. "And King Solomon sent and fetched Hiram out of Tyre. He was the son of a widow of the tribe of Naphtali, and his father was a man of Tyre, a worker in copper. . . . He came to King Solomon, and did all his work. . . . He set up the pillars of the porch of the temple, calling the right pillar Jachin, and the left pillar Boaz. And upon the tops of the pillars was lily-work" (I Kings 7:13, 21, 22). ". . . all the vessels which Hiram made for King Solomon in the Temple of the Lord were of burnished copper. In the plain [kikkar] of the Jordan did the king have them cast, in thickened earthen molds, between Succoth and Zarethan" (I Kings 7:45, 46).

I have found fragments of iron-ore slag on some of the tells north of Adamah and especially upon the site of ancient Succoth. In Solomon's time, this entire district in the Jordan Valley hummed with industrial activity devoted to the turning out of finished metal articles for the adornment of the new Temple. All day long, caravans of donkeys filed down into the valley from the eastern hills, bringing iron ore mined in the Ajlun area and charcoal from the forests of Gilead. Great slag heaps in the vicinity of modern Ajlun, commanding the watershed in which the Wadi Kufrinji rises, testify to the fact that some of the iron ore dug up near there was smelted before being transported down to the Jordan Valley for further refining or remelting and casting.

Most of the copper utilized in Hiram's foundries must have come from King Solomon's copper-mining and smelting sites in the Wadi Arabah. The globules of copper ore obtained there through the charcoal-fueled smelting of crushed cupriferous ores in shallow cavities with the utilization of tuyeres and bellows and also through smelting in pottery crucibles may in part have been remelted into ingot form at King Solomon's industrial, storage, caravanserai and maritime city of Ezion-geber for easier use and/or sale. Many of these copper ingots may of course also have been produced at the Wadi Arabah smelting sites and brought to places like Succoth in the Jordan Valley, as well as to Ezion-geber. Hiram's namesake, the king of Tyre, built and manned with Phoenician craftsmen and sailors the "Tarshish" ships that sailed from Ezion-geber to Ophir. Their cargo probably included copper ingots and copper articles and other products of Israel as articles of exchange. They returned laden with gold and the exotic goods of Arabia, Africa and India (I Kings 9:27–28; 10:1, 2, 10). The very word *Tarshish*, as William F. Albright has pointed out, meant originally "smelter" in Phoenician before it became a place name.[1]

The metal-producing and particularly the metal-manufacturing activities introduced by Solomon on a large scale in the Wadi Arabah and probably at Ezion-geber were repeated on a considerable scale in the Jordan Valley. Plenty of water, close proximity to mines, accessibility to the then-limitless wood supplies for charcoal and nearness to Jerusalem made the region of Succoth the center of widespread smelting and refining and manufacturing activities, without parallel there either before or after the time of Solomon. Clay for molds abounded. The master craftsman Hiram had evidently approved of this part of the Jordan Valley as an area where he could make the most intricate castings.

What a scene must have greeted the eyes of the stranger who during this period visited the east side of the Jordan! Far and wide stretched rich fields of grain, carefully irrigated and continuously tended to see that each acre got its measure of water. In the middle of each large field stood the inevitable watchtower, "like a lodging place in the qusa [cucumber] field"

---

[1] Albright, *Archaeology and the Religion of Israel,* 1956, p. 136; *Bulletin of the American Schools of Oriental Research,* 83 (Oct. 1941), 21–22.

(Isaiah 1:8), where guards were mounted against thieves by day or night. There too the laborers hied themselves at the noon rest hour to eat their loaf of bread, with olives and cheese and fruit in season, and drink their pitcher of water, and then, wrapping themselves in their cloaks and looking like corpses in shrouds, sleep soundly while the flies attacked them in vain. In the midst of these miles of cultivation were many villages, elevated on commanding heights. Clustered about a few of them were smelting furnaces and foundries, aflame with activity, directed by the superior skill of the master craftsman, Hiram of Tyre.

Succoth

Outstanding among the cities located alongside the end-course of the Jabbok was Succoth. The site towered so commandingly above the plain of the Jordan Valley that it could be seen all the way from Adamah, some 8 miles to the south. Succoth is unquestionably to be identified with the prominent ancient mound known today as Tell Deir-alla. How happy Jacob must have been to see it after leaving Penuel on the Jabbok, where he had secured a blessing from the Stranger who had wrestled with him during the night, and forgiveness from Esau, who had become reconciled with him the next day! Following the course of the Jabbok downward, Jacob and his people entered into the fair expanse of a very rich section of the Jordan Valley which in the Bible is known as the emeq (valley) of Succoth. In its midst stood the imposing mound, already ancient in Jacob's time. Here Jacob could rest from his ordeal at Penuel (Tell edh-Dhahab), and here his family could remain for a while, recovering from the hardships of the long journey from Laban's lands far to the northeast. Here was forage for his flocks, land for plowing, water for all. Here he would call a long halt (Genesis 33:16, 17).

All this happened almost four thousand years ago. Jacob moved on to Palestine. Many centuries were to pass before that country was invaded by the Philistines, coming from Mediterranean islands. In the struggle for the conquest of Canaan, the Israelites were finally to win out, but the Philistines were to bequeath it their name. Meanwhile the centrally located Succoth continued to figure in history. Jacob's house and booths disintegrated into dust. Other and more permanent settlers built in his place after him, and they too vanished in time. A new city, still called Succoth, sprang up and flourished, as did all cities in this irrigated valley during any prolonged period of peace. Time passed. There occurred repetitive destruction and rebuilding. Soil and water kept some of the old settlers rooted and attracted new ones.

Excavations at Tell Deir-alla (Succoth) in recent years by H. J. Franken,[2] who prefers to identify it with the Gilgal of I Samuel 13:15, have revealed the presence there of an advanced metallurgical industry for the smelting and casting of copper and iron prior to, during and after Solomon's time. A pottery spout was found, partially disintegrated by heat from the inside, which seems to have been employed to convey molten metal into clay molds (I Kings 7:45–46; II Chronicles 4:17); in fact, a fragment of copper remained inside the spout. Only one bronze vessel was found at Tell Deir-alla, but in a late Iron Age tomb at nearby Tell Mazar a bronze bowl and strainer were recovered. It must be remembered that metal corrodes and disintegrates quickly when affected by moisture.

Franken's most exciting discovery at Tell Deir-alla consisted of three clay tablets bearing inscriptions in a hitherto unknown script. The best preserved of them contains eight words in two registers. The possibility that these tablets, although locally made, may have been inscribed in an Aegaean or Philistine script has been surmised by several scholars.[3]

Throughout the history of Israel, Succoth remained an important place. Solomon had his copper cast in earthen molds all the way from Succoth to Zarethan. Elsewhere the Bible also brackets Succoth and Zaphon, assuming that everybody had heard of them (Joshua 13:27). Finally, about the sixth century B.C., a blight of cumulative exhaustion and conquest hit Succoth, as it did its sister cities in the Jordan Valley. To be sure, during the subsequent Hellenistic, Roman, and Byzantine periods, small settlements established themselves successfully on the mound of Succoth. They in turn flourished and fell, receding into the forgetfulness of the past which had also engulfed their predecessors. Little more than fragments of pottery remained on the surface to testify to their former existence before excavations were undertaken there.

[2] H. J. Franken, "The Excavations at Deir-'alla in Jordan," *Vetus Testamentum*, X (1960), 386–93; XI (1961), 361–72; XII (1962), 378–82; H. J. and C. A. Franken, *A Primer of Old Testament Archaeology* (Leiden: E. J. Brill, 1963), Pls. XI, XIV–XVIIb.

[3] H. J. Franken, "A Bronze Age Shrine and Unknown Script," *The Illustrated London News*, April 17, 1965, pp. 34–35; "Excavations at Deir-'Alla, Season 1964," in *Vetus Testamentum*, XIV:4 (October, 1964), 417–32.

Long before I reached Succoth, I could see it standing like a giant among its lesser fellows in the valley. What would this abandoned mass of houses and cities, risen high like a mighty anthill, be able to tell me? Which of its secrets could still be deciphered? Soon its steeply sloping sides loomed ahead. Around its base gurgled a stream, diverted from the Jabbok River to irrigate some neighboring fields.

Climbing to the top of the mound, which rises about 60 feet above the level of the plain, I found it impossible to take a single step without treading on innumerable fragments of pottery. They were of all shapes and colors, ranging in time through many different civilizations. And as I collected samples of the sherds that littered the surface, it seemed to me that a veritable babel of sound burst out of the depths of the hill. The multitude of voices conveyed no clear meanings to me. I listened hard. Was that a Philistine expression and the other an Israelite phrase? Were those Amorite words, mingled with the accents of Canaanite speech? Did the deep gutturals belong to the still-earlier dolmen-builders or to descendants of the prehistoric men who first peopled this valley? They all seemed to speak at once. Whose voices were those crying out of the depths only to float away into a sea of silence?

Today not a single soul lives on the tell. A few modern graves on the top mark the presence in the vicinity of some tent-dwellers who bury their dead on it and who farm and irrigate a small part of the adjacent fields.

I arranged the sherds I had gathered into separate piles, one group belonging to the time of the Israelites, another to the Late Bronze period that preceded them, a third going back still earlier from the middle of the nineteenth to the middle of the sixteenth century B.C. "Look," I said to my companion Rashid, "look at the beautiful burnished lines on this platter that the ancient potter once proudly turned on his wheel. Look at the even bands of paint encircling this jar, with a band of white slip between them. Look, Rashid, and reflect that these specimens of pottery have outlasted by thousands of years the men and women who made and used them. There were no untilled lands here in ancient days, except when purposely left fallow. Little water was wasted. Men lived in houses of thick mud-brick, crowded within the outer fortification wall. Yes, indeed, they knew how to read and write. On this very mound, perhaps on this particular spot where we are now sitting, was the house of the boy Gideon seized on the outskirts of Succoth, whom he compelled to write down the names of the elders of the city, to their doom.

"Did they believe in God, do you ask, Rashid? Yes, they believed in God. Before the time of the Israelites, the people who lived in the valley believed in many gods. When the Israelites arrived, they brought with them the belief in one God. But only a handful held firmly to this hard-won faith. Prophets and priests had constantly to enjoin the masses to worship God with good deeds and not through offerings, with moral behavior and not through sweet-smelling sacrifices or pious prayers emanating from a complacent certainty that God was on their side. There were also many among them who affirmed belief in the Lord but backslid to the pagan observances of Ashtoreth, trying to straddle two thresholds at one time. As the centuries passed, however, they rejected all gods but God, although many of them worshiped Him ever so imperfectly.

"Yes, Rashid, this God is the same as Allah. This is the God who was worshiped by Moses and Joshua, but also by John the Baptist and Jesus and by Mohammed. He was worshiped here in Succoth, here in the valley of the Jordan. Certainly, all of us can subscribe to what you have just said: Allahu akbar [God is great, and there is none beside Him]. But take no offense, Rashid, if we insist that Mohammed is only one of those who felt His presence more closely than most ordinary mortals. No harm meant, Rashid, but was not Jesus a prophet, and do you Mohammedans yourselves not speak of Nebi Musa, the prophet Moses? Is it not so written in your own Koran? Have you not, indeed, built a shrine to this Nebi Musa on the west side of the Jordan? Let us together say, 'El-hamdu lillah' [Praise be to God] in gratitude for being alive today, and praise Him whom also the makers of some of this ancient pottery worshiped. You and I, Rashid, through the religions that we profess, and through these fragments of pottery that we hold in our hands, link the past to the present. O, Men of Succoth, we, who are rooted in your past, salute your memory."

Succoth was not the only town in the valley of Succoth. It had a number of smaller neighbors, all of them contemporary and some with origins antedating it. Among them is the small mound of Tell el-Ekhsas, the "Mound of Booths." It has been identified by some, mistakenly we think, with the Biblical Succoth, which, as we have already seen, also means "Booths." Tell el-Ekhsas is situated in the center of the Jordan Valley, in the midst of fields still intricately irrigated. Its position is further marked by being above a very slight depression, a little more than a square mile in extent, which is too saline for agriculture. There are no good archaeological reasons why this site should supersede Tell Deir-alla as the location of Biblical Succoth. Its chief claim is the name "Mound of Booths" (Tell el-Ekhas). If this name reflects the ancient one of "Booths"—Succoth—we must remember that it was not an uncommon practice for an ancient place name to shift from an abandoned site to a new one in the vicinity. These changes were particularly frequent in the Hellenistic-Roman period. No other sites in the entire district could compare with Tell Deir-alla in prominence and superiority of location, coupled with surface-pottery evidence of occupation in Biblical times, for identification with Succoth.

V I / Without Biblical names

Wadi Rajeb and Wadi Kufrinji

The identification of Biblical Zarethan

Two of the streams that flow across the east side of the Jordan Valley, cutting it, as if with a cleaver, into distinct sections, are the Wadi Rajeb and the Wadi Kufrinji. By each of these streams is located an extremely important tell. One of them is Tell Qos on the Wadi Rajeb, near the eastern side of the Ghor—Biblical Zaphon, where Jephthah defeated the Ephraimites. The other, farther north, is the striking mound of Tell es-Saidiyeh, near the western end of the Wadi Kufrinji, the Biblical Zarethan. The height on which Zaphon was built marks the upper end of a rich district whose lower limit is fixed by the towering tell of Succoth. From the hills just above to the east came the streams which conditioned their existence and prosperity. Comparable in importance to Zaphon and Succoth, but directly overlooking the Jordan at the western edge of this east side of the valley, were Adamah and Zarethan.

Zarethan is the site which figures in the Biblical account of the Israelites' crossing the Jordan on dry land, when the wall of water which dammed up the river reached from Adamah as far as the fortress of Zarethan (Joshua 3:16). It is mentioned too, as we have seen, in the description of Solomon's industrial activities in the Jordan Valley (I Kings 7:46; II Chronicles 4:17).

But how, on the basis of the two scanty references in the Bible to Zarethan, can it be identified with any particular one of the numerous bleak, uninhabited, long-abandoned tells in the Jordan Valley? There are dozens of sites to choose from, dozens of nameless corpses of Biblical cities to confound speculation. In the verse which merely mentions the casting of copper vessels between Succoth and Zarethan there is no hint as to where Zarethan might be, or even in what direction to look for it. However, a good deal of information can be squeezed out of Joshua 3:16, which speaks of the wall of water reaching from Adamah as far as the fortress of Zarethan.

If we were pleading the case in court to restore to Tell es-Saidiyeh its legal name of Zarethan and the associated historical heritage, we would argue as follows:

a. First of all, it is clear that Zarethan could not be south of Adamah, because the water downstream from Adamah stopped running, and had indeed backed up as far north as Zarethan, according to the Biblical description. Furthermore, there are no Biblical sites south of Adamah for a considerable distance. Nor would Zarethan be west of Adamah—that is, on the west bank of the Jordan, as has been maintained by some—because to say that the wall of water extended from the east side to the west side of the river would not be saying anything. Naturally, it reached all the way to the western bank of the river, because otherwise the water would have continued to flow southward and the crossing on dry land could not have been affected.

b. All the Biblical verses that speak of the areas between Succoth and Zarethan and between Adamah and Zarethan refer to sites in the eastern half of the Jordan Valley, and list them from south to north.

c. In view of the configuration of the Jordan Valley proper, the Ghor ("Depression"), the upper level, which is about 125 feet above the lower level ("thicket") of the Zor, or "Jungle of the Jordan," through which the river flows, Zarethan would have to be close enough to and immediately overlooking the Zor of the Jordan to make it possible to say that the wall of water extended from Adamah to Zarethan. If Zarethan were situated in the center of the upper level of the valley or near its eastern hills, neither the much-lower-situated Jordan River nor its wider bed, the "Jungle of the Jordan," could ever be seen from it. I have seen fighter planes skimming along at high speed low over the Zor, hidden from sight below the wild hills that border its banks and invisible to anyone standing in the Ghor valley proper well above the deep trough of the river and its banks.

d. Zarethan would have to be situated by some source of water, preferably by the side of one of the streams that flow across the east side of the valley to empty finally into the Jordan.

e. It seems obvious that Zarethan must have been a well-known landmark, the equivalent of a Dan or Beersheba elsewhere, because otherwise it would not have been mentioned in the Bible, which listed only places of obvious historical or topographic importance. In this connection, it must have been so important a settlement that when a Jerusalemite, for instance, heard of it, he could say to himself, "Yes, I know where it is."

f. It is likely that a place like Zarethan would have been occupied not only in the time of the Israelites, when the Bible was written, but also much earlier, when the same physical factors making for its importance were present.

g. Finally, the pottery found on the logical site would have to conform to the periods in history when it is known to have been occupied, to judge from such evidence as is contained in the Bible or in other ancient records.

The actual archaeological facts agree completely with the conclusions to be derived from a careful examination of Joshua 3:16. This verse was meant to be taken literally, to the effect that the Jordan River was dammed up from Adamah as far as Zarethan, enabling the Israelites freely and easily to cross on dry land to the west side of the Jordan. There is only one place in the entire Jordan Valley that meets these specifications, and that is the site of Tell es-Saidiyeh.

Tell es-Saidiyeh is situated about twelve miles north-northeast of Adamah. It is on the east side of the Jordan, being only about a mile from it, on the edge of the Ghor part of the valley, which overlooks the Jordan and its Zor, or "Jungle." Immediately below the north side of Tell es-Saidiyeh is the Wadi Kufrinji, which empties into the Jordan. And it is just at this point, below the north side of the long, high mound, that several fine springs appear, further to swell the volume of the stream of the Wadi Kufrinji. East of the tell stretches a wide and fertile reach of the Jordan Valley. The waters of the Wadi Kufrinji are partly used to irrigate some of the rich adjacent lands. After emerging from the hills to the east, it cuts a clear although shallow path for itself on its way across the valley to the Jordan, and serves as a boundary between the areas to the north and south of it.

There are other ancient sites along the Wadi Kufrinji, east of Tell es-Saidiyeh, but none is of great importance. Tell es-Saidiyeh is the outstanding mound in this entire section of the valley. From the hills to the east it can be seen looming up in the distance like a strong citadel—which is just what it was. The mound guards the approach to western Palestine and commands the width of the rich valley east of it. People in the hill country on both sides of the Jordan could not but have known of it. And the large quantities of sherds found on it show not only that it was densely inhabited in Israelite times, but also that it had been occupied previously as early as the late Chalcolithic-Early Bronze II periods, extending from the thirty-fifth to the twenty-sixth centuries B.C. No place in the Jordan Valley meets the requirements for identification with Zarethan as well as Tell es-Saidiyeh does.

There is striking confirmation of this conclusion. In the third century A.D. there lived a learned man in Palestine who described the relative positions of Adamah and Zarethan as 12 miles distant from each other. He was Rabbi Johanan, whose words are recorded in the Talmud, which is full of important topographic allusions. He could easily have known the actual site of Zarethan, whose Biblical name had apparently not yet been forgotten in his day.

Excavations at Tell es-Saidiyeh by James B. Pritchard in 1963, 1964 and 1965 have yielded results in full accord with our suggested identification. Copper vessels found in a twelfth-century-B.C. tomb, and other finds such as two bronze swords from a warrior's tomb, bear out the correctness of the Biblical statements to which we have previously referred, mentioning the casting of copper vessels in thickened earthen molds between Succoth and Zarethan (I Kings 7:46; II Chronicles 4:17). The Israelite-period city of Tell es-Saidiyeh was surrounded by a strong casemate-fortification wall. It also possessed an underground tunnel, related to the type found in Jerusalem, Gezer, Megiddo and Qir of Moab (Kerak), for example, giving the inhabitants safe access to a water supply inside the fortification confines even under siege circumstances.

*W*adi *Yabis*

Jabesh-gilead

Among the six smaller perennial tributaries between the larger ones, the Yarmuk and the Jabbok, that flow into the Jordan from the east—the rivers Arab, Ziqlab, Jurm, Yabis, Kufrinji and Rajeb—the one that indirectly receives most attention in the Biblical narrative is the Wadi Yabis. It is never mentioned by name, but incidents and individuals and places connected in one way or another with the Wadi Yabis are frequently referred to. The Biblical names of all these six streams elude us, although we regard it as most likely that the Israelites knew the Wadi Yabis as the Nahal Jabesh-gilead.

The stream of the Wadi Yabis, which is north of the Wadi Kufrinji, races through a deep canyon before it reaches the level of the Jordan Valley. With blessed tenacity, it has clung in modern form to its ancient name, which must have been the River Jabesh or the River Jabesh-gilead; "Jabesh" has a familiar ring to our ears. Does not the Bible speak frequently of the town Jabesh-gilead on the east side of the Jordan Valley? Had not cruel punishment once been meted out to its residents for failing to join the expedition against the tribe of Benjamin, some of whose members had mishandled the Levite's concubine? The town was put to the sword, with only four hundred virgins being saved. Through some strange quirk of tribal justice, they were thereupon given to the decimated tribe of Benjamin to replenish its numbers (Judges 21:8–14). And, on another occasion, had not the men of Jabesh-gilead been saved through the intervention of Saul from having their right eyes put out by Nahash the Ammonite as a lasting "reproach upon all Israel" (I Sam. 11:1–13)? This demonstration on Saul's part of a far-reaching responsibility for fellow Israelites was a kindness (stemming from a sense of mutual *hesed*, family relationship and responsibility) the men of Jabesh-gilead were not soon to forget.

Saul's star, and with it Israel's fortunes, rose fast but fell even more suddenly. The long-drawn-out struggle between Israel and the invaders from the sea resulted in a temporary victory for the Philistines at the Battle of Gilboa near Beth-shan. "And the battle went sore against Saul, and the archers overtook him.... Then said Saul to his armorbearer, 'Draw your sword, and thrust it through me, lest these uncircumcised ones come and do it and abuse me.' But his armorbearer would not, for he was sore afraid. Therefore Saul took his sword and fell upon it. Whereupon ... his armorbearer ... too fell upon his sword and died with him. So Saul died, and his three sons, and his armorbearer, and all his men, the same day together.... And it came to pass on the morrow, when the Philistines came to strip the slain, that they found Saul and his three sons fallen on Mount Gilboa.... And they cut off his head, and stripped off his armor.... And they put his armor in the temple of Ashtaroth; and they fastened his body to the wall of Beth-shan" (I Samuel 31:3–10).

News travels fast in the almost self-contained Jordan Valley. Wherever we camped in it south of the Sea of Galilee, we knew from passing travelers practically within the day what had transpired at Beisan. And so it was in ancient times, only more so, because there were then more people and more activity in the Jordan Valley. Certainly within a few hours after Saul's body had been shamefully impaled on the city wall of Beth-shan, news of the indignity had spread far and wide in the valley. And no village there was more vitally concerned with what had happened to Saul than Jabesh-gilead, which was located southeast of Beth-shan on the east side of the Jordan.

One of the Jabeshites had probably been in Beth-shan during the morning, had witnessed the degrading spectacle and had writhed at the Philistine indignities. That afternoon he returned home and related how he had seen the corpses of the princes of Israel staked out like slain animals. The elders tore their cloaks and capped their heads with dust. The entire population made loud lament. Was there nothing to be done? "Men of Jabesh-gilead," one of their leaders could well have said, "can we allow the bodies of our brothers to rot under another day's sun, be devoured by vultures and be stoned and spit at by these Philistine dogs—may God blot out their memory!" All agreed instantly that it was their obvious duty somehow to rescue the corpses and give them honorable burial.

Darkness fell. Chosen groups of men sallied forth from Jabesh-gilead, moved northward, forded the Jordan and climbed the broad benches of land which rose like great steps to the top of the Plain of Beth-shan. They knew every track that led up to the great citadel and every narrow twisting alley inside it. Somehow they gained access to the city, where they had relatives and friends. Perhaps the Philistines, flushed with victory, were not keeping careful watch that night. Stealthily the Jabeshites slipped through the shadows and clambered over the battlements of the outer fortification wall. Silently, speedily, they cut loose the bodies of their benefactors and lowered them to some of their companions waiting below, who wrapped the corpses in shrouds brought for the purpose.

Now for the journey homeward. Willing hands carried the heavy burdens in changing shifts. They recrossed the Jordan, climbed up from the "Jungle" to the Ghor level of the valley proper, and some hours later were back at Jabesh-gilead. Having left just after dark, they had returned before dawn. The gates of the fortress on top of its high hill were swung open to receive them, after they had first purified themselves. The bodies were left outside and later burned clean of the defilement they had suffered. After that, the bones were wrapped in the finest cloth available, and then, to the accompaniment of the singing of sad psalms, interred under a sacred tree in the nearby cemetery. The men of Jabesh-gilead had acquitted themselves honorably. To the best of their ability they had repaid the debt they owed the noble dead who, while living, had once saved them from shame worse than death.

"And when the inhabitants of Jabesh-gilead heard . . . what the Philistines had done to Saul, all the valiant men arose, and marched all night, and took the body of Saul and the bodies of his sons from the wall of Beth-shan; and they returned to Jabesh [that very same night], and burnt them there. And they took their bones, and buried them under the tamarisk-tree of Jabesh. After that, they fasted seven days" (I Samuel 31:11–13). Later, when David was anointed king in Saul's place, he sent a special message to the inhabitants of Jabesh-gilead, promising to hold them in high regard for this act of *hesed* faithfulness to Saul. "And David sent messengers unto the men of Jabesh-gilead, and said unto them, may the Lord bless you for showing this *hesed* fealty to Saul, your lord, by providing him with honorable burial. . . . And I also will requite you this kindness" (II Samuel 2:5, 6).

The tamarisk tree of Jabesh has of course long since disappeared, but the ancient site and the memory of the devoted sense of brotherly obligation of its citizens still endure. It is appropriate that the part of the site of

Jabesh-gilead where the remains of Saul and his sons may have been buried should today be called Meqbereh, "a burial place." But unfortunately for the romantically minded, there is hardly a single ancient site in the entire Jordan Valley that has not been utilized by modern Arabs to bury their dead.

Late one afternoon my Circassian companion, Rashid Hamid, and I rode up to the tents of the Zeinati Arabs, pitched near the point where the Wadi Yabis enters the Jordan Valley. For generations, explorers had sought the site of Jabesh-gilead, looking for it, correctly enough, along the Wadi Yabis, the River Jabesh. Would we be any more successful? Tribesmen ran out, seized the reins, and begged us to dismount. In Mohammed Zeinati's absence, his youngest brother came forward to meet us and to lead us to the places of honor near the fireplace in the great guest tent. The coals were blown on to start a fresh flame, and more fuel of twigs and dried dung was added. Already one of the slaves had roasted some coffee beans and was pounding them with the pestle, striking a rhythmic beat in the mortar. He was preparing the bitter brew that the Arab host invariably offers his guest and himself sips at intervals all day long. Then sweet tea was served, together with a light snack in anticipation of the *dhabiheh,* the sheep slaughtered the moment after we appeared, that would be served to us later in the evening.

As soon after our arrival as decorum permitted, and before the be-numbing evening meal had to be attacked, I directed the conversation to the subject of ancient ruins. The assembled company assured us that there was nothing in the region that would interest us, thinking we would be attracted only by great above-surface ruins, standing pillars such as the great Corinthian columns in Jerash and the like. It was hard to make them understand that any little mound with fragments of pottery on it came within our concern. I felt certain that somewhere in the immediate vicinity of the encampment itself, with the fine stream of the Wadi Yabis issuing forth from the nearby hills to make possible the irrigation of hundreds of fine acres of rich valley land, there were bound to be found ancient Biblical and pre-Biblical sites. Hereabouts should be the site of Jabesh-gilead itself! One could almost figure out and mark on a map the theoretical position of Jabesh-gilead on the east side of the Jordan Valley, merely by a careful perusal and checking of the Biblical accounts dealing with it.

For example, when Saul's army relieved Jabesh-gilead from the siege by Nahash the Ammonite, it marched first to Bezek, at the edge of the hills overlooking the Jordan Valley from the west. Descending at night into the valley and fording the Jordan, Saul's men reached Jabesh-gilead in the early watch of the morning, made a surprise attack upon the unsuspecting Ammonites and utterly defeated them. This story, which there is no reason to disbelieve, clearly indicates that Jabesh-gilead was on the east side of the Jordan Valley, so near to the point of departure at Bezek that the march and surprise attack could be made under cover of darkness in the course of one night.

Furthermore it could be assumed that Jabesh-gilead would be located by some source of water, and in this instance certainly alongside the Wadi Yabis. The area to be examined was considerably lessened by this consideration. Had Jabesh-gilead been situated farther east, where it had previously been thought to be, in the hills above the valley, Saul's strategy would have had to be completely different. He could not then have reached his goal in one night's march, or have attacked under cover of darkness. By the same token, if Jabesh-gilead were located somewhere in the eastern hills, even though overlooking the Wadi Yabis, it would have been impossible for the men of Jabesh-gilead to receive the news of the infamy perpetrated on the bodies of Saul and his sons, and on the same day bring them back to Jabesh-gilead for burial. Clearly, then, Jabesh-gilead had to be in the valley proper, on the east side of the Jordan, by the side of or immediately above the Wadi Yabis and within a comparatively few miles of Beth-shan.

All these things ran through my mind as I sat in the tent of Mohammed Zeinati and sipped coffee served by his chief black slave, Ibn Ihmeid Abdul-Heir. It was about an hour before nightfall when we went out to walk up and down in front of the tent and "breathe the air," as the Arab expression goes. About half a mile to the east I espied a low, insignificant-looking mound, which might have been natural but which resembled the low knolls, slightly lighter in color than their surroundings, that experience had taught me to recognize as ancient sites. I asked my companions whether or not it had a name. "It is called Tell el-Meqbereh," they replied. "Tell el-Meqbereh?" I echoed in pleased surprise. "The Tell of the Burial Place?" Sometimes, to be sure, a place may be called a tell and not be an antiquity site at all, as, for instance, Tell Sleihat south of Tell el-Meqbereh. Tell Sleihat is a high, completely isolated, imposing-looking hill which has the typical flattish top and sloping sides characteristic of many artificial tells. It is, however, a completely natural hill, as I can testify from a meticulous examination, repeated on several occasions. Normally, however, if a place is called a tell, there is every reason to assume that it is an artificial city-hill, formed by successive towns each built on the ruins of the preceding one.

It was all I could do to refrain from rushing over immediately to Tell el-Meqbereh and commencing to search for the fragments of pottery which reveal the ages of occupation on a site as clearly as tree rings disclose the age and life-history of a tree. As soon as possible, early the next morning, we mounted our horses and rode over to the site. Our most sanguine hopes were fulfilled. Large quantities of sherds of all kinds were found, many of them belonging to Israelite times from about the thirteenth to the sixth centuries B.C., with others going as far back, approximately, as 3200 B.C.—to the beginning of the Early Bronze Age.

It was like springtime in the Jordan Valley when we first visited Tell el-Meqbereh in the month of December. The fields round about the low mound were lush green with growths of all kinds. Flocks of sheep and herds of goats and cattle, belonging to the well-to-do Zeinati Arabs, grazed there all day long. Part of the nearby land was being plowed for the spring planting. Oxen and camels were pulling pointed sticks of plows edged with iron across the fields. And it could have been an inhabitant of ancient Jabesh-gilead who was supervising the entire activity instead of one of the relatives of Mohammed Zeinati. The planted fields would be irrigated at the proper time by the waters of the Wadi Yabis that flowed almost immediately below the south side of the mound. The pastoral scene, with its Biblical aspect, lent lifelike quality to the slumbering site of Tell el-Meqbereh.

Several hundred yards east of Tell el-Meqbereh a high flat-topped hill stands alone, like an advance sentinel of the slopes that mount steeply to the broken plateau of northern Gilead. The bare sides of this hill, cultivated only at the very bottom, soon rise abruptly for some distance, revealing great ribs of rock, stripped naked of all covering of soil. A mean track leads up to its top, which we found had once been completely surrounded by a great stone wall. Large sections of this outer fortification could still be traced. Despite a luxuriant growth of weeds, a considerable quantity of sherds was found, duplicating those picked up at Tell el-Meqbereh. Indeed, we had first been led to the examination of this isolated hill by reason of a broad trail of fragments of pottery which seemed to connect it with Tell el-Meqbereh. Questioning revealed then that the anciently occupied hilltop was called Tell Abu Kharaz. It completely dominates the Wadi Yabis, which, after leaving its deep gorge in the eastern hills, moves westward across the valley to the Jordan. There is a fine view from Tell Abu Kharaz as far as Beisan and Tell el-Husn, the mound of ancient Beth-shan, and the distance between them can be walked in a few hours. Actually, Tell Abu Kharaz and Tell el-Meqbereh must be considered one site, the latter being the residential section of the great fortress towering directly above it. This double site is definitely the only one which agrees with all the Biblical data concerning Jabesh-gilead.

That night we stayed in the tent of Aref Zeinati—Mohammed Zeinati having moved his camp some distance away—pitched in the Jordan Valley, close to the Wadi Yabis and directly across from the hill surmounted by the ruins of the ancient fortress of Jabesh-gilead. I told the story of its past to the assembled Arabs who sat around the fireplace in the tent. It is possible, although most unlikely, that in their veins some of the blood of the men of Jabesh-gilead still flows. They cultivate the same lands. They lead much the same lives. The interest of my listeners was so keen, their questions so to the point, that soon I almost forgot to whom I was talking. Were these the Arabs of Zeinati, or were these the Israelites of Jabesh-gilead? It was all I could do to refrain from turning to one of them and asking him how the men of Jabesh-gilead had got past the Philistine guards on the city wall of Beth-shan on that memorable night! Or had none been posted that evening? To an archaeologist who can, so to speak, quicken the artifacts of bygone civilizations with the breath of life, there is frequently no perceptible difference between what was and is. Events and people and places, not of days or years, but of centuries and millennia, have a tendency to telescope themselves in his thinking.

Abel-meholah

From Jabesh-gilead we followed the Wadi Yabis upstream eastward into the hills of Gilead. Soon we were forced to abandon its direct course by the steepness of the canyon walls. Descending from the broken plateau, we came to a bend in the stream where, long ago, the rushing waters had cut down the hills to make a little valley which is still carefully cultivated and irrigated. Grain grows richly there, and small groves of lemon and fig trees flourish, yielding much fruit in season. Overlooking this hidden garden area is a large hill, called Tell el-Maqlub. On it is an extensive ancient settlement. The hill is cultivated from bottom to top in roughly terraced benches, planted largely to grain. There are vineyards in the vicinity. Around the top of the hill can be seen clear vestiges of a strong outer wall. Further traces of extensive occupation were furnished by quantities of pottery fragments, strewn over the top and sides of the hill, belonging mainly to Iron Age I–II (thirteenth to sixth centuries B.C.) and to the later Hellenistic, Roman and Byzantine periods. There were also numerous earlier sherds dating from Early Bronze I–II (thirty-second to twenty-sixth centuries B.C.) and perhaps somewhat earlier, and others belonging to the first part of Middle Bronze II (nineteenth and eighteenth centuries B.C.).

Tell el-Maqlub had sometimes previously been identified with Jabesh-gilead, not because of its pottery, for which earlier explorers never looked, but because it was located by the Wadi Yabis. The great double site of Tell Abu Kharaz and Tell el-Meqbereh had escaped attention. Nor did these explorers consider that news from the Jordan Valley penetrates but slowly and accidentally into the highlands of Gilead and their isolated villages, of which Tell el-Maqlub was one. Its residents might not have learned for days what had transpired at Beth-shan. The highlanders now dwelling near Tell el-Maqlub know practically nothing of what goes on at Beisan in the Jordan Valley. The seminomadic Arabs who live farther north in the Jordan Valley, however, know within a few hours what happens at Beisan. In addition, from Tell el-Maqlub to Beisan is a good six or seven hours' walk each way. The men of Tell el-Maqlub could scarcely have reached Beth-shan and returned, carrying the bodies of Saul and his sons, in the course of one night.

If, however, Tell el-Maqlub is definitely not to be identified with Jabesh-gilead, there is much reason for identifying it with Biblical Abel-meholah. The name Abel-meholah wandered in the abbreviated form of Abel during the Hellenistic period to a nearby site marked today by an Arab village still known as Kefr Abil. The main historical importance of Abel-meholah lies in the fact that it was the home of Elisha the Prophet. Like Elijah, he too was a native of Transjordan. Hitherto, however, the site of Abel-meholah had been located by everybody on the west side of the Jordan, largely because of a completely erroneous identification made by the ancient historian Eusebius (A.D. 260–340). He identified it with Beth-maela, ten miles south of Scythopolis (Beth-shan), apparently on the basis of vague similarity of names.

Everything points to the fact that Abel-meholah was a hill city and not a lowland town. It would have been much more to the point had attention been paid to the simple sense of Abel-meholah, which means the "Vale of Dancing," than to attempt impossible philological comparisons. One is reminded of the Benjaminites, who hid in the vineyards at Shiloh and seized the maidens for wives when they came out to dance the dances (*meholah*) of the grape festival (Judges 21:20, 21). And one recalls furthermore the defeat Jephthah inflicted upon the Ammonites, smiting them from Aroer as far as Abel-keramim, the "Vale of Vineyards." These places were situated by running streams of water and in hilly country devoted to the cultivation of the grapevine. There are numerous similar areas in Transjordan today, such as those around Salt, Naur, Sweileh and Suf, where grapes have been grown for thousands of years. The name Abel-meholah, the "Vale of Dancing," may have originated from the hilly vineyard country where it was situated, and where at harvest-time the grape festival was celebrated with joyous dances. Tell el-Maqlub is ideally situated for the location of Abel-meholah. And it would have been at Tell el-Maqlub that Elijah stopped to see Elisha on his way north from Horeb in Sinai to Damascus in Syria.

The Brook Cherith

Elijah had fled to the sacred mountain in Sinai to escape the wrath of Ahab's wife, the Phoenician princess Jezebel. The prophet had been instrumental in confounding and destroying at Mount Carmel the prophets of her god, Baal. At Sinai, Elijah had been enjoined to depart on a three-fold mission: to travel to Damascus, where he was to help to crown Hazael king of Syria; in his own country to anoint Jehu king of Israel; and finally to consecrate Elisha as his successor. He was able to accomplish only the last of these tasks, it being left to Elisha to complete the first two (II Kings 8:7–15; 9:1–13). The very undertaking by Elijah of this journey spelled the coming of age of Israelite prophecy: it was henceforth in increasing measure to stress that all affairs of men were the concern of God. And the true prophet was to function not as an onlooker and even less as a professional soothsayer, but as an agent of God's moral order. Neither war nor politics nor private affairs were to be outside the scope of prophetic concern. The man of God was to speak the Word of God regardless of consequences to himself, zealous only to obey the categorical imperatives of divine law and revelation.

The road to the homes of Elisha and Hazael led through Transjordan in virtually a straight line from one to the other. Jehu was finally anointed king at Ramoth-gilead, which we have identified with Tell Ramith in northern Transjordan, near the Syrian border. (Excavations there by Paul Lapp seem to have confirmed the identification.) The first stage of his journey led Elisha to his native haunts, where Elijah too was at home. After all, was not Elijah a native of Jabesh-gilead, a few miles below and to the west of Abel-meholah in the Jordan Valley? A small scribal error has crept into the Biblical text, causing much confusion with regard to Elijah's birthplace, although it has always been abundantly clear that he came from the east side of the Jordan. He is described in I Kings 17:1 as "Elijah the Tishbite, of the *toshabe* Gilead," which is usually translated as "Elijah the Tishbite, of the sojourners of Gilead." That is vague to the point of exasperation. The correct reading, restoring Elijah to his proper background, should probably be: "Elijah the Jabeshite, from Jabesh-gilead."

In this connection, it is perhaps now possible to clear up another mystery with which the account of the life of Elijah has long been burdened—the location of the famous Brook Cherith. Here again there has been much confusion, because scholars as well as novelists have not paid sufficient attention to the literal meaning of the Biblical text. Continuing the story which commences with the mention of "Elijah the Jabeshite of Jabesh-gilead," as we have slightly emended the text, the Biblical narrative reads: "And the word of the Lord came unto him [Elijah], Depart from here and turn eastward and hide yourself by the Brook Cherith, that is [east of] the Jordan. You shall drink from the brook, and I have commanded the ravens to feed you there. So he went and did according to the word of the Lord, dwelling by the Brook Cherith, that is [east of] the Jordan. And the ravens brought him bread and meat in the morning, and bread and meat in the evening; and he drank from the brook. After a while the brook dried up, because there was no rain in the land" (I Kings 17:2–7). It is explicitly stated in the text that when Elijah went to hide himself by the side of the Brook Cherith he went eastward (in Transjordan toward the desert).

The prophets ever turned to the stern simplicity of the desert. They sought to perpetuate the clear-cut standards of brotherhood and belief in God which had first come into the consciousness of Israel during its desert days. Twice in his lifetime Elijah sought refuge in the desert, first of Transjordan and then of Sinai. In later centuries Paul of Tarsus was to turn to the eastern desert to renew his strength. For three years he stayed in the desert before re-entering the arena of the world at Damascus.

The Brook Cherith was undoubtedly a small wadi, usually with some water in it but drying up on occasion. It may well have been one of the easternmost branches of the River Jabesh, whose roots extend into the desert. There Elijah hid himself from the wrath of Ahab of Israel. Afraid of nought save the God he served, Elijah had promised Ahab that divine punishment would be visited upon him for his waywardness in worshiping Baal and Ashtoreth in his capital city of Samaria. He foretold a famine in the land of Israel. "As the Lord, the God of Israel, liveth, before whom I stand, there shall not be dew nor rain these years, but according to my word" (I Kings 17:1). Elijah fled then to the Brook Cherith, near the desert east of his home at Jabesh-gilead. As a youth he had probably shepherded flocks there in the springtime after the early rains.

It cannot definitely be proved that the Brook Cherith is in or near the eastern beginnings of the River Jabesh. One thing, nevertheless, is beyond debate. The Brook Cherith is emphatically not to be identified, as for instance by George Moore in his magnificent novel *The Brook Kerith*, with the Wadi Qelt that runs from below Jerusalem to Jericho and then across the west side of the valley to the Jordan. The Brook Cherith is just as certainly on the east side of the Jordan as are Abel-meholah and Jabesh-gilead.

Elijah's way to Abel-meholah to find Elisha was an easy one for him. He could almost have gone there blindfolded from Jabesh-gilead, which he would probably have visited first, en route from the valley to the hills of Gilead. After all, he had spent his childhood and youth along the reaches of the Jabesh, knowing exactly where the best grazing lay for his father's flocks, and at what times of the year to lead them there, and when to shepherd them toward the stream to drink their fill. But from another point of view this was the most difficult journey Elijah had ever undertaken in his life. Nearing the end of his career, he was about to lay the mantle of successorship upon his disciple Elisha. The future belonged to his pupil. His own day was almost over, and the time for his departure from this world had arrived.

"So he [Elijah] departed thence, and found Elisha the son of Shaphat, who was plowing, with twelve yoke of oxen before him, and he with the twelfth: Elijah passed by him, and cast his mantle upon him. And he left the oxen and ran after Elijah and said unto him, Let me, I pray you, kiss my father and my mother, and then I will follow you. And he said to him, Go back again, for what have I done to you? And he returned from following him, and took the yoke of oxen, and slew them, and boiled their flesh with the yokes of the oxen and gave to the people and they ate. Then he arose, and went after Elijah and ministered unto him" (I Kings 19:19–21).

When I visited Tell el-Maqlub, the *fellahin* were engaged in plowing on both sides of the adjacent perennial stream of the Wadi Yabis with just about a dozen yoke of oxen all told. A simple Arab peasant halted his team of oxen to greet me and to answer my questions about the countryside. Was there any connection, however tenuous, between him and that other peasant who long centuries before had been plowing in his place?

The last act in the life of Elijah was yet to take place. And where else but along the east side of the Jordan, where his life had begun? From Gilgal on the west side of the Jordan to Beth-el in the hills near Jerusalem, and again from Beth-el past Ai down to Jericho in the valley below, Elijah traced a pilgrim's circle, accompanied by his disciple Elisha, whom he could not persuade to leave his side. "Elijah the Jabeshite is here," was the common cry as soon as he was seen. Who did not know by sight or reputation "the hairy man girt with a girdle of leather about his loins" (II Kings 1:8)? And who was not aware that this would be his last visit and that this was a last leavetaking? Finally the two men stood again by the Jordan, and they crossed over to the east bank. There the pupil prayed for a double portion of his master's spirit, and he received the blessing for which he asked.

In what vivid terms is described the departure of Elijah from the world of laborious effort to the heavenly sphere of miraculous happenings! "And these two [Elijah and Elisha] stood by the Jordan. Then Elijah took his mantle and rolled it up and struck the waters, and the water was parted, till the two of them could go over on dry ground. When they had crossed, Elijah said to Elisha, Ask what I shall do for you, before I am taken from you. And Elisha said, I pray you, let me inherit a double share of your spirit. And he said, You have asked a hard thing: yet, if you see me as I am being taken from you, it shall be so for you; but if you do not see me, it shall not be so. And it was while they were still talking that behold a chariot of fire and horses of fire separated the two of them; And Elijah went up by a whirlwind into heaven. And Elisha saw it, and he cried, My father, my father, the chariots of Israel and its horsemen!" (II Kings 2:7–12).

Elisha thereupon assumed the burden of prophecy, recrossing the Jordan and carrying on in the footsteps of his master. "And when he [Elisha] saw him no more, then he took hold of his own clothes and rent them into two pieces. And he took up the mantle of Elijah that had fallen from him and went back and stood on the bank of the Jordan, . . . and struck the water, saying, Where is the Lord, the God of Elijah? and when he had struck the water, the water was parted leaving a crossing open; and Elisha went over. Now when the sons of the prophets who were at Jericho saw him, they said, The spirit of Elijah rests on Elisha. And they came to meet him and bowed themselves to the ground before him" (II Kings 2:12–15).

Wadi Jurm

Pella

Occasionally one finds references to ancient Jordan Valley villages in records much earlier than the time of Elijah and older than the Bible and in accord with the evidence of pottery remains. Such records exist in the form of Egyptian name lists and cuneiform tablets. Most of the latter have hitherto been found in Egypt, but they were written in the Babylonian tongue and cuneiform script by Palestinian and other western Asiatic rulers to two of their Egyptian overlords. These el-Amarna records (named after the place of their discovery at el-Amarna—ancient Akhetaton—two hundred miles south of Cairo on the east bank of the Nile) date mainly from the early fourteenth century B.C. In one of them is a message from a Canaanite princess with the resounding title of Lady-of-the-Lions, written apparently to Amenophis IV. In it the place of her residence is mentioned as being at Sapuna, which is the equivalent of the Biblical Zaphon (Tell Qos).

In another of the el-Amarna letters, mention is made of Pihilu, later to become known as Pella and now called Tabaqat Fahil. Crossing the swiftly flowing Wadi Jurm at the point of its entrance into the valley, one gazes upward to the great fortress mound of Tabaqat Fahil situated high in the hills, like an eagle's nest on a ledge. It occupies a unique position with regard to the Jordan Valley, being neither part of it nor completely separated from it. Winding past this site of ancient Pella is a track, once good enough to carry chariot traffic and donkey trains. In the Roman period it helped connect Pella with its confederated cities of the Decapolis, of which it was an outstanding member. The steep slopes above Pella lead down, at the east end of the shelf on which it is situated, into a caldronlike hollow. Along its sides there gushes forth a whole series of strong springs, sweet and clear, forming within a few hundred yards a rushing stream that plunges headlong down to the floor of the valley. It was inevitable that men should settle by this gathering of waters, and build houses and temples and strong fortifications. It seems likely that someday there will be found in the vicinity some settlements contemporary with earliest Natufian and Neolithic Jericho (ca. 7000 B.C.).

When we first visited Tabaqat Fahil, we were met and were entertained at lunch by Dhiab Suleiman, the mukhtar (headman) of the village. It mattered not that he was poorly clothed, his house small, his people povertystricken. It mattered not that the humblest building in ancient Pella must have been a mansion compared to any of their rude dwellings. We were exchanging polite conversational amenities with a prince of Pella. We drank his coffee, which slaked our thirst. We dipped pieces of his fragrant, freshly baked bread into a dish of sour milk and ate the eggs he boiled and peeled for us. We exclaimed honestly over the goodness of it all. Inwardly we hoped that his family would not go hungry that day because of this drain on their slender store of supplies. We could under no circumstances have refused his hospitality or hurt him with pity for his poverty. I have forgotten many splendid feasts, but I shall never forget the bread we broke with Suleiman. The invitation to his board was a royal summons, and we commoners had no choice but to obey. I photographed him, his hand resting on a fragment of fine Corinthian capital with which his children had been playing in the courtyard. Then he guided us about the ruins, and we explained to him the significance of some of them: Roman bastions, Byzantine church foundations, medieval glazed Arabic pottery. He exclaimed over the age of the sherds, variously belonging, as we told him in Arabic, going backward in time, to Arabs and Byzantines, to Romans and contemporaries of the people of Musa (Moses) and to others still earlier of the time of Ibrahim (Abraham).

Between the Jabbok and the Wadi Nimrin

Between the Jabbok and the Wadi Nimrin on the east side of the Jordan is an arid region about sixteen miles long, with neither springs nor streams to moisten its dryness. Its acres could not be made productive in the past, and people had no reason to congregate in towns or hope for survival if they did. Rain occurs only in occasional years. When it does fall, the short-lived grass that springs up magically in its wake is quickly cropped to its roots by hungry flocks and herds of Bedouins' sheep and goats. Stone circles, revealing the tenting places of such shepherds, go back in part to high antiquity. For many long centuries the land there was vacant, in sharp contrast to the once-populous and intensively tilled parts of the Jordan Valley north and south of it.

This condition was changed in small part when the dynamic Romans came along and the push of growing populations in the Near East became so strong that every available inch of ground had to be utilized if possible. On the basis of hundreds of ancient sites discovered by our archaeological survey, I estimate that the population in Transjordan during the Roman and equally populous Byzantine periods amounted to about a million and a quarter. In those days, as we have seen, the soil was sacred. It was tended with a loving care that helped to preserve it from one generation to another. Hillsides were terraced at the cost of great toil. Forests, covering large stretches of the country, were carefully preserved, with conscious or unconscious concern for their irreplaceable values. Dams, reservoirs, and cisterns without number were built to conserve the available water supply. Aqueducts spanned the land. Even underground water supplies were tapped.

The Romans did not despair of utilizing part of the desert section of the Jordan Valley between the Jabbok and the Nimrin streams. At one point someone noticed a trickle of water at the bottom of the gentle slope that led across the valley from the base of the hills on its east side. A ditch

ABOVE: Head of a Semitic king or deity from el-Medeiyineh, Moab. *Nelson Glueck*

BELOW: Heads of figurines from el-Medeiyineh and Baluah, Moab. *Nelson Glueck*

BELOW: Hieroglyphic inscription of Sethos I, from the fourteenth century B.C., found at Beth-shan. It describes the nipping in the bud of a revolt in the Beth-shan area against Egyptian rule

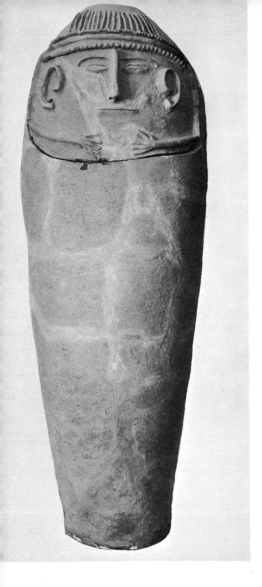

LEFT: Pottery coffin of twelfth century B.C. from Beth-shan, made by Aegean mercenaries there.

BELOW: Besalt statue of Ramesses III, twelfth century B.C., found at Beth-shan

RIGHT: Snake-decorated pottery from Beth-shan, twelfth century B.C. *James B. Pritchard, The University Museum*

146

ABOVE LEFT: Neolithic clay figurine with stylized face, raised head and elongated eyes, Sha'ar ha-Golan. *Courtesy of Israel Department of Antiquities*

ABOVE: Neolithic stone figurine, Sha'ar ha-Golan. *Courtesy of Israel Department of Antiquities*

RIGHT: Shell-eyed head of Neolithic cult-statue from Jericho, modeled in plaster about 7000 years ago

ABOVE: Yarmukian pottery, Sha'ar ha-Golan, Neolithic. *Courtesy of Israel Department of Antiquities*

RIGHT: Neolithic decorated pebble, Sha'ar ha-Golan. *Courtesy of Israel Department of Antiquities*

LEFT: Crude ivory fertility figure from Chalcolithic Safadi, about 3500 B.C. *Courtesy of Jean Perrot, Mission Archéologique Française en Israel*

BELOW: Basalt Bowls, ivory sickle, figurine, head and decorated piece, Chalcolithic Safadi. *Courtesy of Jean Perrot, Mission Archéologique Française en Israel*

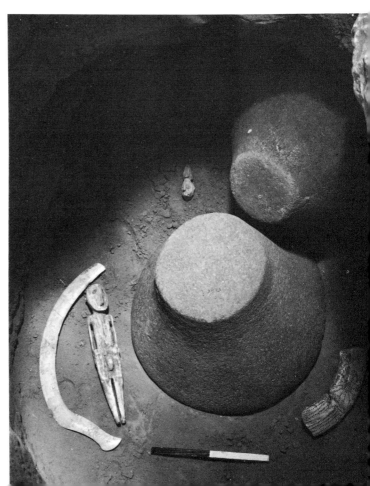

ABOVE AND BELOW: Figurine from el-Meshhed, near Mt. Nebo. *Nelson Glueck*

ABOVE: Ivory fertility figure, Chalcolithic Safadi, near Beersheba, about 3500 B.C. *Courtesy of Jean Perrot, Mission Archéologique Française en Israel*

PRECEDING PAGE: Chalcolithic bronze ornamented "crown" from near the Nahal Hever, excavated by P. Bar-Adon. *Courtesy of Israel Department of Antiquities*

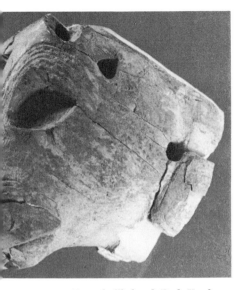

ABOVE: Ivory bull's head, Beth-Yerah, about 2600–2400 B.C. *Courtesy of Israel Department of Antiquities*

RIGHT: Pottery figurine of mother and child from Beth-Yerah, third millennium B.C. *Courtesy of Israel Department of Antiquities*

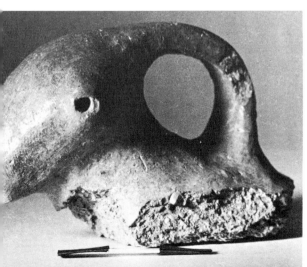

LEFT: Mouth and handle of zoomorphic juglet, from Beth-Yerah, about 2600–2400 B.C. *Courtesy of Israel Department of Antiquities*

LEFT: Nelson Glueck examining Middle Bronze I pottery from the time of Abraham. *Nelson Glueck*

BELOW: Bowl of Khirbet Kerak ware from Beth-Yerah, dating about 2500 B.C. *Courtesy of Israel Department of Antiquities*

ABOVE: "Jericho John" and his mirrored profile. An anthropomorphic vase from seventeenth-century B.C. Jericho

RIGHT: Chalcolithic ossuary from Azor, near Tel Aviv. *Courtesy of Jean Perrot, Mission Archéologique Française en Israel*

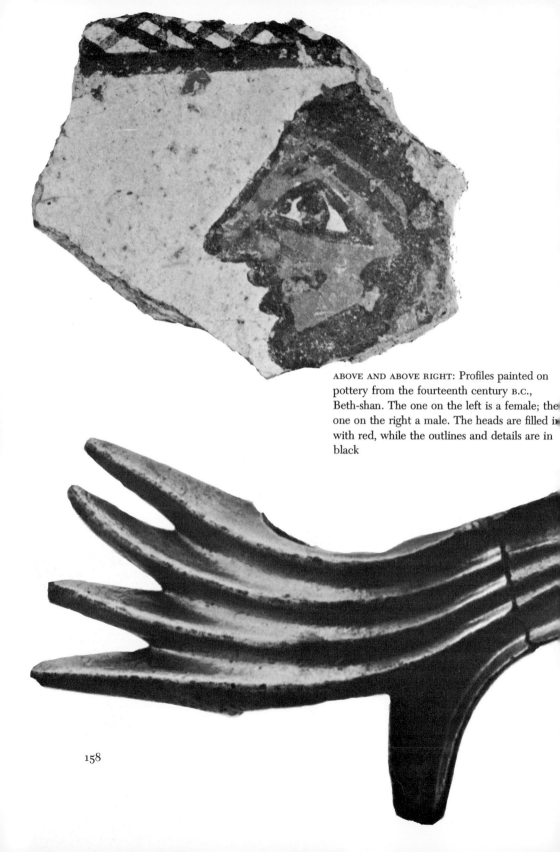

ABOVE AND ABOVE RIGHT: Profiles painted on pottery from the fourteenth century B.C., Beth-shan. The one on the left is a female; the one on the right a male. The heads are filled in with red, while the outlines and details are in black

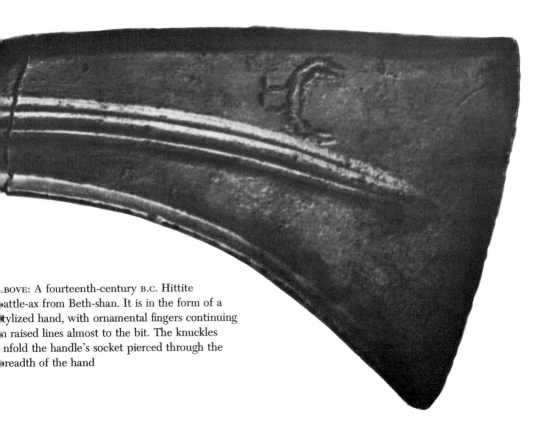

ABOVE: A fourteenth-century B.C. Hittite
battle-ax from Beth-shan. It is in the form of a
stylized hand, with ornamental fingers continuing
in raised lines almost to the bit. The knuckles
enfold the handle's socket pierced through the
breadth of the hand

ғᴛ: Lion-dog panel, dating to
e fourteenth century B.C., from
th-shan

ᴏᴠᴇ: Prehistoric elephant's
sk from the Jordan Valley

ɢʜᴛ: Neolithic plastered skull
m Jericho. *Courtesy of Dr.*
thleen M. Kenyon

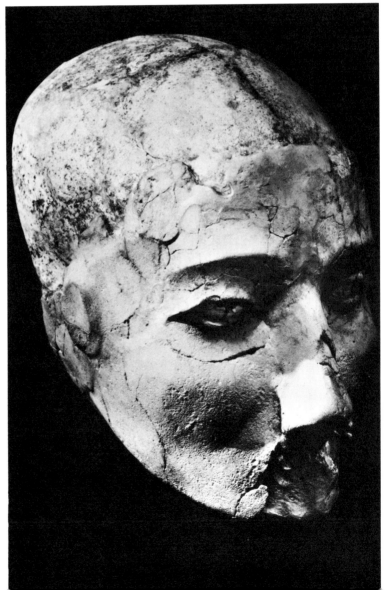

BELOW: Bronze bowl with smaller bowl, strainer and juglet as they were found fused together in a woman's tomb at Zarethan. *Courtesy of Dr. James B. Pritchard, The University Museum*

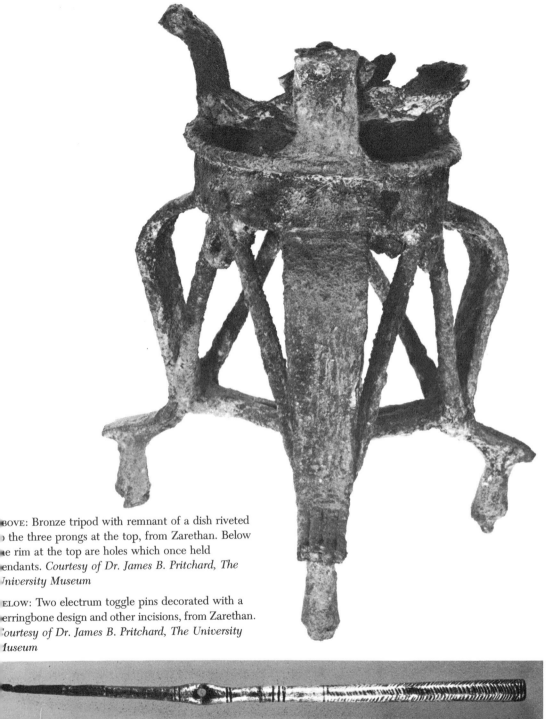

ABOVE: Bronze tripod with remnant of a dish riveted
to the three prongs at the top, from Zarethan. Below
the rim at the top are holes which once held
pendants. *Courtesy of Dr. James B. Pritchard, The
University Museum*

BELOW: Two electrum toggle pins decorated with a
herringbone design and other incisions, from Zarethan.
*Courtesy of Dr. James B. Pritchard, The University
Museum*

ABOVE: Egyptian Bubastite cat amulet, enlarged, from Tell el-Kheleifeh (Ezion-geber). *American Schools of Oriental Research*

LEFT: Stucco statue of a girl with flowers, from Khirbet Mefjer, north of Jericho, where the Umaiyads, early Mohammedan Arabs, built a resplendent palace in the eighth century A.D.

RIGHT: Stucco figure of a fox (?) eating grapes, from Khirbet Mefjer

BELOW: Decorated pottery jug from a Byzantine villa at Beth-shan. *Courtesy of Israel Department of Antiquities*

RIGHT: Atargatis as grain goddess, from Khirbet Tannur

RIGHT BELOW: Stucco figure of helmeted man, from Khirbet Mefjer

NEXT PAGE: Part of Flood story in mosaic floor of Byzantine synagogue at Jerash

was dug following the course of the seepage of water, and the farther the ditch went the greater the quantity of water obtained. Soon the ditch was too deep to be continued without its walls collapsing or without widening it, which apparently proved to be impractical. By then it had occurred to the venturesome engineer in charge of operations that he had struck an underground water table. He proceeded to have a series of vertical shafts dug down to the water table, and these were connected by a tunnel to each other and to the ditch previously dug. Thus, at the bottom of each shaft, a certain amount of water was collected from the spongy earth about it. The water flowed then by gravity through the horizontal tunnel to the bottom of the next vertical shaft slightly below it, and so on till finally it emerged into the ditch as a strong stream, capable of irrigating numerous fields. All that was necessary thereafter was to keep the tunnel and the shafts that led into it free of debris. No hoisting or pumping was necessary. Imagine the elation of the engineer who first pioneered this project. Water obtained in the desert by striking its rock!

Government engineers of the Hashemite Kingdom of Jordan rediscovered this artesian system. Attention was directed to the same trickle of water that attracted the attention of the Roman engineer, and at the same time to a long line of filled-in pits leading down the gentle slope from east to west. The pits were cleared, the interconnecting tunnel found and opened and the whole system restored to use. Gardens now flourish in this desert, where no cultivated plants had thrived since the Byzantine period.

Similar artesian wells, known today as *qanat* or *fuqara*, have been found elsewhere in the Near East, hailing back probably at the earliest to Roman and Byzantine times. Their use is still widespread. Little wonder then that the Bible says nothing of this parched area on the east side of the Jordan Valley. During the Nabataean, Roman and Byzantine periods, between particularly the second century B.C. and the sixth century A.D., dynamic populations pushed out into marginal lands where no permanent, sedentary civilizations preceded or followed them. By skillful and persistent conservation of the occasional rainwater, and where possible by wise cultivation and care of the soil, they were able to survive, often even to flourish, in arid and semiarid areas, which long since then have been practically empty of settled inhabitants.

VII / On the west side of
the Jordan

Paths of pilgrims

The west side of the Jordan Valley is narrower and much less watered by perennial streams than the east side. It is neither so full of settlements nor mentioned so frequently in the Bible. Now two and a half tribes, requiring special consideration, were separating themselves on that side from the rest of Israel. But there too, wherever water was to be had with which to irrigate land, men gathered together in sedentary communities, tilling the soil from early prehistoric times onward. To cross over the Jordan into the Promised Land to the west had required a long struggle. The Jordan Valley has long been the path of pilgrims. Several of its cities achieved outstanding importance and lasting fame. Most of its inhabited places remained nameless in the Bible. The names of a few were preserved only in earlier records, as that of Rehob, for instance, mentioned in an Egyptian stele of the fourteenth century B.C. found at Beth-shan. Some of the Cisjordan Valley (*Cis*, on this side, as opposed to *Trans*jordan, the other side of the Jordan) sites were large, and, despite the silence of the Bible, must have been well known in their day. Others the Bible could not be expected to mention, because they had ceased to exist several thousand years before its first pages were written.

Pass along the length of the west side of the Jordan and take notice of the large tells which jut above the level of the landscape, many of them clearly visible from the eastern side. There is the massive Tell edh-Dhiabeh, looming over a widened section of the Zor, situated several hundred yards west of Jisr Sheikh Hussein and anciently controlling both the way across the river and the pass leading to the Plain of Esdraelon. It is paralleled on the eastern side of the Jordan by a site almost equally large, called Tell Sheikh Mohammed, occupied especially in the eighteenth to seventeenth centuries B.C. A strong spring gives rise to a flowing stream which irrigates the fields in front of Tell edh-Dhiabeh. Behind it to the west is a series of low ridges rising to the level of the valley proper. The flattish top of the mound presents an extraordinary sight. Its surface is pockmarked with a maze of shallow pits, as though it had been invaded by an army of moles digging for cover and throwing up behind them all manner of objects. Around each pit we found masses of fragments of brilliantly painted band-slip ware. Many pieces were so large that even a novice could visualize the complete pottery vessel to which they belonged. Large ledge-handles and fine pieces of pattern-burnished juglets were strewn about among numerous other sherds. The pottery picture was as clear as could be, representing a very distinctive period of settlement in Early Bronze Ia, dating to the last quarter of the fourth millennium B.C. The pottery of Tell edh-Dhiabeh is not alone in its kind either in the Jordan Valley or elsewhere.

This pottery was characteristic of a widespread civilization which flowered for only a few centuries. Finally some disaster overcame it, making desolate mounds of its inhabited sites, many of them never again to be settled. The ancient remains of Tell edh-Dhiabeh have been disturbed in modern times by fellahin, who stored their surplus grain in pits sunk into the dry earth on the top of the mound. They dug into a rich deposit of pottery, which had been left in houses of long ago destroyed in some terrible catastrophe. The pottery survived, because nothing short of crushing it into powder could make it unrecognizable, so enduring are well-baked wares.

A few hundred yards behind Tell edh-Dhiabeh, on a knoll to the west, are pottery remains of a small Israelite settlement of the Early Iron Age. This settlement came into being some 2,000 years after the Early Bronze Age site of Tell edh-Dhiabeh was destroyed. Beside it today has grown up the modern Jewish settlement of Maoz. The ancient Israelite site has lost the name that distinguished it in Biblical times, and there are many others in the same dilemma, deprived by time of their individual identities. There is, for instance, the small but strategically located Tell el-Mazar, which dominates the point where the widening Wadi el-Farah merges with the Jordan Valley. A perennial stream flows down this wadi, which in a small way parallels the larger river Jabbok on the opposite side of the Jordan. The sherds picked up on the slopes of Tell el-Mazar indicate that it was occupied in Israelite and pre-Israelite periods, as well as later, but there is no clue to its name in Biblical times.

In the Jordan Valley, in the neighborhood of Beth-shan, there are numerous satellite towns whose early identity likewise escapes us. It is possible, however, to fix the general periods of their occupation by the fragments of pottery found on them. North of Jericho, by the Wadi Auja et-Tahta and between the latter and Tell el-Mazar, are still other sites occupied in the Israelite period and in much earlier and later times.

Beth-shan (Scythopolis)

The anonymity which has cloaked almost all the ancient settlements on the west side of the Jordan and whose importance, to our way of thinking, might well have warranted their being mentioned in the Bible did not extend, fortunately, to its two outstanding cities. They were Beth-shan in the north and Jericho in the south. These names have been preserved down to our day, when the Arabs still know them as Beisan and er-Riha and the modern Israelis as Beth-shan and Jericho. Outstanding as these two were, the strong fortress of Hazor, overlooking the west side of the Jordan River south of Lake Huleh, put to the sword and burnt by Joshua (Joshua 11:10, 11), was larger than either.

The situation of Beth-shan was such that any settlement located there had to become the leading city of an important district. Several strong springs and the waters of the perennial Jalud irrigate a fertile soil into rich fecundity. The climate is subtropical. The outstanding mound, known today as Tell el-Husn, the "Fortress Hill," dominates the Jordan Valley at one of its widest and most fruitful parts. It guards the Jordan end of the great highway which, following the length of the Plain of Esdraelon, connects the Mediterranean coast and the Nile Valley with Mesopotamia. The counterpart of this great fortress near the western end of the highway was the stronghold of Megiddo, later known as Armageddon and now called Tell el-Mutesellim.

It is like turning the pages of a thoroughly documented and fascinatingly interesting book of history to follow the course of the excavations conducted at Tell el-Husn. Beneath more modern accumulations were found the ruins of the period of the Crusades, during which the town was so thoroughly destroyed that thereafter it never regained its former prosperity. The present Israeli village of Beth-shan, a short distance from the tell, cannot yet measure up to the proud cities which preceded it, superimposed upon each other on the original hill site. Beneath the Crusaders' masonry lay the fallen fort, mosque and dwellings of the Arabs who completed their conquest of the entire land in A.D. 640, a few years after the death of Mohammed in 632. The never-forgotten ancient name of Beth-shan then replaced the comparatively new name of Scythopolis, by which it had been known to the Greeks, Romans and Byzantines. That name may perhaps hark back to the seventh century B.C., when the warlike Scythians of Indo-European origin, originally at home on the plains of southern Russia, swept southward as far as the boundaries of Egypt.

It has been suggested that the name Beth-shan means "Temple of the Serpent-god." Be that as it may, among the most interesting finds there were numerous representations of serpents, one with human breasts and a milk bowl placed beneath them. Beth-shan may have been a center of the serpent cult, which was widespread in ancient Palestine. One recalls the serpent stele found by Albright at Tell Beit Mirsim (Kiriath-sefer or Debir) in southwestern Palestine, and the presence of the Nehushtan, the copper serpent, which may have been in Solomon's Temple in Jerusalem. There was also the copper serpent made by Moses in the Arabah (Numbers 21:9).

The curved walls and mosaic floors of a magnificent circular Byzantine cathedral of the sixth century A.D. were found there. Underneath it were the remains of a rectangular basilica of early Christian times. Across the valley, north of the tell, was a sixth-century-A.D. Byzantine monastery, with elaborate mosaic floors featuring harvesting and hunting scenes, many kinds of birds and a complex representation of the zodiac. The Christian buildings had replaced pagan temples of the Roman and still earlier Hellenistic periods. Among the ruins of these temples were the remains of one dating to the second or third centuries B.C., which was probably dedicated to the god Dionysus. Indeed, the town was sometimes named Nysa, after his birthplace. In 107 B.C., the Jewish high priest and ruler John Hyrcanus gained control of Scythopolis. It remained under Maccabaean rule until 64 B.C., when Palestine became a Roman province. Under the Romans the city flourished mightily. It soon became the chief city of the Decapolis, that league of ten cities with Graeco-Roman culture among which we have already mentioned Gadara, Pella, Gerasa (Jerash) and Philadelphia. The existing ruins of Gerasa help us visualize what Hellenistic-Roman Scythopolis, Gadara, Jericho, Caesarea Philippi and other contemporary cities looked like.

In earlier centuries the Philistines and Israelites had fought bitterly for possession of the vitally strategic point of Beth-shan, as it was then known. For a while toward the end of the eleventh century B.C., the Philistines won out. It was then that "they put his [Saul's] armor in the temple of Ashtaroth and fastened his body to the wall of Beth-shan" (I Samuel 31:10). Subsequently the Israelites seized the site and held it for several centuries.

The deepest imprint upon Beth-shan was left by the Egyptians, who controlled Palestine during the second half of the second millennium B.C. Anthropoid sarcophagi, made in imitation of Egyptian originals, have been found there. A whole series of Egyptian temples, inscriptions and statues has come to light at Beth-shan in levels belonging to the period of Egyptian occupation, demonstrating how strong an interest the Egyptians had in the city. But Beth-shan was a cosmopolitan center, and other cultural influences were operative there, even during the time Egyptian influence was predominant. Northern Syrian or northern Mesopotamian influence is represented by the lion relief from the Mekal temple belonging to about the fourteenth century B.C. An axe and dagger of Hittite design, Syro-Hittite cylinder seals, and a small bronze figure that seems to represent Teshub, the Hittite storm-god, suggest Hittite influence during the period of Rameses II, in the thirteenth century B.C.

The excavations have shown that the site had already been settled in the late Chalcolithic period, at approximately 3500 B.C., and was continuously inhabited after that. Flip the pages and get a moving-picture impression of the actors crossing the stage of history at Beth-shan. Among them were Canaanites, Egyptians, Hittites, Babylonians, Philistines, Israelites,

Scythians, Persians, Greeks, Romans, Byzantines, Arabs and Crusaders, and now Israelis. And remember, the play has just begun!

Jericho, the home of history

The Walls of Jericho

Of the two cities Beth-shan and Jericho, the latter has become the more famous. History was at home there. The story of civilization might well start with the words: "And in the beginning there was Jericho." It stood at the edge of the hills, in the midst of fragrant gardens and verdant fields, irrigated into glowing greenness by the unfailing waters of the Wadi Qelt. Immediately below the rise on which it stood was the strong spring now known as Ain es-Sultan and also as Elisha's fountain. Lordly palms afforded abundant shade and succulent dates in season. Pomegranate and olive trees flourished, and a heady wine was made of grapes that ripen early in the subtropical heat. I have on a December day sat and soaked up the sunshine in Jericho, then driven to Jerusalem an hour later to shiver in wintry blasts there. However productive the land around the city, nothing has ever grown in the weird crisscross of chalky *qattarah* hills that form a cruel belt of no man's land between the carefully planted acres of the Plain of Jericho and the wild Jungle of the Jordan below it.

Jericho drew men to it like a magnet. The goddess of the moon, to whom it was early dedicated, blessed it with unrestrained bounty. Its citizens grew rich and rotund. Its women flowered fast and married young. It is true that they withered early, like tender grass under the glare of a burning sun, but while their youth and strength lasted they spent them prodigally. Their main pride lay in the sons they mothered. Of daughters there was always a sufficiency for all purposes, for wives and fieldworkers, for concubines and courtesans. The trade of the latter was less sicklied over with sanctity than that of their sisters who functioned as sacred prostitutes in the shrines of Astarte. To the unhallowed guild of women for hire belonged Rahab. She plied her trade in her house on top of the great mud-brick wall which engirded the fullness of the rich Canaanite city of Jericho. How were the ponderous elders to know that in her frail hands would someday lie its destiny?

A crisis familiar to its past history once again confronted Jericho. Its pattern was known even to the children. Had they not from infancy been frightened by tales of the wild men from the East who rode out of the desert like a fiery wind to ravage and plunder, destroy and burn? Always behind the opulence of Jericho lurked the fear of the raiders from Arabia, attracted to its riches like flies to honey. Their lean hunger could never be fattened, and their appetite seemed to grow with feeding. The chronicles of Jericho were replete with accounts of beating them back, buying them off, or being overwhelmed by them. More often than one cared to recall, they had come with careful calculation just at harvest-time and had besieged the city until they had filled their bellies with grain they had neither sown nor reaped, eaten the fruit of trees they had not tended, and carried off what they could not consume. They would then retreat into the desert fastnesses where they could not be followed, leaving behind them the taunting assurance that they would return again in another year.

The danger that threatened Jericho this time was the most serious within the memory of any of its inhabitants. This was not the usual enemy that launched a sudden attack and then beat as sudden a retreat. This was an inundating flood. Would the walls of Jericho be sufficiently strong to stem it? Counsel was taken. Increased stores of food were stocked. All available fighting men were gathered together. The defenses of the great mud-brick wall were examined and, where necessary, repaired and strengthened. Thousands of bricks were required for the purpose. There was a flurry of activity as mud was mixed with straw and pressed into rectangular wooden forms, and as the completed bricks were set out, row upon row, to dry in the sun. But it was all in vain. The city was doomed, by treachery from within, by strategy and strength from without. There was to be no withstanding of the Bene-Israel awaiting on the other side of the Jordan the signal to advance.

The commander, Joshua ben-Nun, encamped at (Abel) Shittim in the Plains of Moab at the northeast end of the Dead Sea, which could be seen across the river from Jericho, had sent out two men to look over the land and reconnoiter Jericho itself. They had found their way to the house of the harlot Rahab. Theirs was a dangerous mission, and what better hideout in the town itself, and where better could they make inquiries about it, than in her home? Rahab yielded her favors for reward, and grabbed her gain where she could find it. She bore no love in her heart for her townsmen, who used her in private and avoided her in public. And would she ever forget the whispers of their wives and children, which often reached her ears as she passed them: "There goes Rahab the harlot!" She hated them all. The time had come when she could both have her revenge and save her skin. The two spies were speedily traced to her house. She hid them under the flax spread out to dry on its flat roof while she sent their pursuers on a wild-goose chase after them to the fords of the Jordan. "Yes, the men came unto me, but I knew not whence they were: and it came to pass about the time of the shutting of the gate, when it was dark, that the men went out; whither the men went I know not: pursue after them quickly; for you will overtake them.... And the men pursued after them the way to the Jordan unto the fords" (Joshua 2:4–7).

Earthy woman of the world that she was, Rahab was well informed of the progress of the Bene-Israel through Transjordan, and she was convinced that nothing could stay their advance and that Jericho must fall before them, like all the other cities which lay in their path. Back she sped to the roof, to make her terms with the two strangers whose lives were now in bond to her. She would help them escape if they would guarantee to save her life and the lives of her family when Jericho fell to the Israelite army. "I know," the Biblical account reports her as saying, "that the Lord has given you the land, and that the fear of you is fallen upon us, and that all the inhabitants of the land melt away before you. For we have heard how the Lord dried up the water of the Red Sea before you, ... and what you did to the two kings of the Amorites, that were beyond the Jordan, to Sihon and Og, whom you utterly destroyed.... For the Lord your God is He who is God in heaven above, and on earth beneath" (Joshua 2:9–11). The men agreed. "Our life for yours," they said, "if you do not tell this business of ours" (Joshua 2:14), and they gave her a scarlet cord to put in her window as token of security for her household when the attack came. "Then she let them down by a rope through the window: for her house was built into the city wall, and she dwelt in the wall" (Joshua 2:15).

Excitement ran high in the camp of the Bene-Israel on the east side of the Jordan. With considerable anxiety, Joshua awaited the return of his two scouts. His people were ready to march. It would not do to delay the attack much longer. Death and hunger and weariness had long been their familiar companions. That was now all behind them. The struggle to reach the Jordan was still a subject for campfire retelling, but no more than that.

Finally Joshua received the intelligence report about Jericho for which he had sent his scouts. It was favorable to his plans. The inhabitants were frightened and dispirited. There were friends within the city itself. So forward, warriors of Israel! The tents were struck. The whole camp moved. The host reached the Jordan, the priests with the Ark in advance. And then the wonder occurred. The river became dammed up, ceasing to flow from Adamah southward. The people of Israel passed over on dry land. Taking twelve stones out of its bed, they set them up in Gilgal, on the west side of the Jordan facing Jericho, as a memorial of this divinely blessed adventure.

The news of the crossing of the Jordan had filled the inhabitants of Jericho with terror. "Now Jericho was shut up from within and from without, because of the Bene-Israel: none went out, and none came in" (Joshua 6:1). The strategy of the defenders was to sit tight and trust to the massive defenses of their great city wall. Should the enemy approach too closely, he would be showered with arrows and darts, and doused with boiling oil in case he ventured still nearer. But the tactics of the invaders were of a different order. For six days they encircled the city, while the weakhearted there grew faint with fear and internal dissension mounted. Clamorous grew the cries for submission while there was yet time, for coming to terms with the Israelites who were crowned with the halo of invincibility, and whose march westward had been marked by one miracle after another.

Meanwhile Rahab sat secure in her house. One by one she had gathered her family to her perch, whispering to each: "There is no hope for you save in my care. There is no hope." And soon the whisper was echoed in every house and had penetrated the fastness of every heart: "There is no hope. There is no hope." The battle was really over before it had begun. The Bene-Israel had but to batter at the gates and the great bastion would fall like an overripe fig. Indeed, this was the order of the battle for the seventh day. The priests were to blow the trumpets and the people to shout great shouts and, under the intoxication of the tumult, to attack. The conclusion was a foregone one. Jericho was bound to fall. The stars were set in their courses against her. The very earth was disturbed to its depths. It trembled, and the firm wall of Jericho fell flat. The city was suddenly bared even of all semblance of defense.

"So the people shouted and trumpets were blown. As soon as the people heard the sound of the trumpet, the people raised a great shout, and the wall fell down flat, so that the people went up into the city, every man straight before him, and they took the city" (Joshua 6:20). Mindful of the promise to Rahab, they brought her and her family to safety in the camp of Israel, whereupon "they burned the city with fire" (Joshua 6:24). "Joshua laid an oath upon them at that time, saying, Cursed be the man before the Lord, that rises up and rebuilds this city Jericho: At the loss of his first-born shall he lay its foundation. And at the cost of his youngest son shall he set up its gates" (Joshua 6:26).

So once again Jericho was destroyed, although it cannot as yet be archaeologically verified, as it had been so often in its long history. A veritable Babel's tower of towns had sprung up over the original knoll by the time of the last Canaanite city, which the treacherous Rahab betrayed. The most recent ruins were soon mercifully buried under a thin cover of dirt brought by the winds. For several centuries no new town was built on top of the tell until finally, in the ninth century B.C., Hiel of Bethel braved Joshua's ban and suffered the consequences of his curse. "In his [Ahab's] days Hiel of Bethel built Jericho: he laid his foundations at the cost of Abiram his first-born, and set up its gates at the cost of his youngest son Segub, according to the word of the Lord, voiced by Joshua ben-Nun" (I Kings 16:34).

Delving deeply into the mound of ancient Jericho, known today as Tell es-Sultan, archaeologists have found remains reaching back for many millennia. In one sector, at the northeast corner, they dug through 80 feet of the debris of seventeen settlements before sterile soil was reached. Starting at the top and going downward in space and backward in time, the strata of these settlements have been numbered from I to XVII. They carry the history of man at Jericho from the thirteenth century B.C. as far back as the Late Natufian period of the Mount Carmel caves, more than 10,000 years ago.

The first settlers at Jericho left behind them very delicate, tiny flints called microliths. These minute blades and other tools required the most careful craftsmanship. They were inserted into wooden or bone shafts to form sawlike blades and are characteristic of the prehistoric Natufian period, which came to an end nearly ten millennia ago. The stages of expanding civilization were now to succeed each other rapidly. It was not long before those who followed the microlith-makers learned to build permanent houses of considerable excellence. Fourteen superimposed floors, composed of clay and lime, pounded firm and painted and polished dull red, have been excavated in one of these houses belonging to the Pre-Pottery Neolithic Jericho B, which may be dated approximately between the middle of the seventh and the middle of the sixth millennia B.C. Each house in turn, after its destruction, served as a foundation for the one subsequently built upon it. By the time the walls of the topmost one collapsed, there had been added to the original height of the mound some 20 feet of debris, consisting of strata XVII to IX.

In one of the levels of Pre-Pottery Neolithic Jericho A (ca. 7000–6500 B.C.), there were some small clay figurines of goats and sheep and other domesticated animals, in addition to other objects including models of male organs. Were they symbols of some early fertility cult? They were found in and around the remains of a building that had a large inner chamber, a wide antechamber and a portico originally supported by six wooden posts. In stratum IX, of the early Pottery Neolithic level, dating from approximately 5000 to 4500 B.C. and extending down into the earlier stratum X, was found an instructive clay model of a house. It looked like a beehive, with a rounded conical roof of the type that can be seen today in some parts of Syria and Mesopotamia. With a floor of stone slabs over a thick base, it was 40 inches high and 30 inches wide. A doorway was meant to be closed by rolling a round flat stone into place. There was a second story occupying the upper third of the building, supported by a central pillar, with another pillar supporting the domed roof.

The early houses, whose walls were made of beaten earth (pisé) or of plano-convex, "hogback," adobe bricks were a far cry from the cave dwellings of the Palaeolithic period. But an even farther cry was the sculptor's atelier in stratum X of Pre-Pottery Neolithic Jericho B, in which some amazing works of art remained. It is true that the medium was clay, the technique crude, the product primitive, but the sculptor fashioned his figures with artistic imagination and power. They were built up on a framework of reeds. One head in particular has been preserved almost intact. It was formed to show the full face. One forgets when looking at it that the head is actually flat, having little more depth than necessary to mold the face. The sightless stillness of the deeply impressed shell eyes, the ridged eyebrows, aquiline nose, prominent cheeks, lines of paint representing tattooing or hair, or both, and the thin line of mouth above a somewhat protruding lower lip, combine to lend a quality of impersonal but strong reality to this primitive sculpture. It is like a death mask of someone who had been vibrantly alive. Remains of a pair of legs, one of them bent gracefully at the knee, were also recovered. It is not impossible that the flat, shell-eyed head was part of the same feminine (?) figure to which these legs, modeled in the round, belonged. Several groups of sculptures were found, representing apparently an early triad of god and goddess and offspring.

It must be remembered that these figures were fashioned about eight thousand years ago. Civilization was developing by leaps and bounds in the Jordan Valley. Almost two millennia later, highly complex and brilliantly ornate frescoes with religious themes were painted at the nearby Chalcolithic settlement of Teleilat Ghassul, located in the Plains of Moab beyond the northeast end of the Dead Sea.

Another type of sculpture from Pre-Pottery Neolithic Jericho B consisted of plastered skulls with shells as eyes and bands of paint on the head. They slightly preceded in time and were closely related in character to the flat-faced, almost two- rather than three-dimensional heads of the statues of the above-mentioned triads of deities. These plastered skulls (denoting probably the existence of a mortuary cult) were found beneath the floors of houses in a form of burial that goes back to the Natufian period and ceases with the advent of the new culture of the Pottery Neolithic period of Jericho.

Actual human skulls were employed. Over their bone structure the features of the dead were faithfully reproduced in clay plaster, with detailed representation of nostrils, ears, eyelids and mouth. The likenesses of individual human beings were created, with painted clay instead of the original flesh, and bivalve or cowrie shells instead of the original eyes.

The Pre-Pottery Neolithic Jericho, with a population estimated by its excavator, Kathleen Kenyon, to have been over 2000 by the seventh millennium B.C., was a fabulous town in many respects, whose like is not yet known elsewhere. The Pre-Pottery Neolithic Jericho A city, which was built about 4000 years before the construction of the earliest of the Egyptian Pyramids, was surrounded by an enormous defensive wall faced with stones, some of them weighing several tons. Originally over 23 feet high and rebuilt several times, and enclosing an area over half a mile in diameter, this great fortification-wall was surrounded by a dry moat 23 feet wide and 10 feet deep! This huge defense wall was built about 9000 years ago, preceding the construction of any other known fortified sites by many millennia. The fortifications of Pre-Pottery Neolithic Jericho were further strengthened by at least one massive round tower. Access to the top was gained by a staircase along an internal shaft, with the small outer entrance at the base easily blocked from the inside.

Irrigation agriculture alone, as Emmanuel Anati has suggested, however extensive it may have been in the environs of Pre-Pottery Neolithic Jericho, may not have provided sufficient economic basis to support a city of its size and create the wealth and power reflected in its massive fortifications. Extensive trade may have contributed to the extraordinary growth of this great city. Found in it were obsidian tools, probably from Anatolia, lamps of turquoise matrix from Sinai, cowrie shells from the Mediterranean, in exchange for which and other imported products Pre-Pottery Neolithic Jericho may have paid in part with agricultural products and also with salt and bitumen from the Dead Sea, sulphur from the Jericho plains and balsam and perhaps spices grown in its gardens or at places like Ain Gedi on the west side of the Dead Sea or even imported from distant Arabia.

Other equally ancient sites existed, many of them in the Jordan Valley, paralleling or filling in present gaps in the history of early Jericho across the span of Mesolithic Natufian, Pre-Pottery and Pottery Neolithic to Chalcolithic and beyond. Here we may mention Natufian Enan on the west side of the Huleh Valley, excavated by Jean Perrot; Beida, five miles north of Petra, discovered and excavated by Diana Kirkbride, which is contemporary with Pre-Pottery Neolithic Jericho A; Munhatta, close to Kibbutz Gesher, on the west side of the Upper Jordan Valley, excavated by Jean Perrot and Nehemiah Tsuri, filling a gap in the last half of the sixth millennium B.C. between strata X and IX of Neolithic Jericho and extending also to the subsequent Yarmukian Shaar ha-Golan period, plus the considerably later Early Bronze Age (paralleling Beth-shan XVI–XVII); Shaar ha-Golan near the confluence of the Yarmuk and the Jordan, excavated by Moshe Stekelis, assigned to ca. 4500–4250 B.C. by William F. Albright in the Pottery Neolithic period between Jericho IX and VIII; and Tell Eli, near Shaar ha-Golan, at the confluence of the Wadi Fejjas and the Jordan, to the southeast of the Sea of Galilee, excavated by Moshe Prausnitz and dating from Early Pottery Neolithic (Jericho IX) of the first half of the fifth millennium B.C. to the Chalcolithic of the first two thirds of the fourth millennium B.C.

The artists who created the triads of shell-eyed figures in Pre-Pottery

Neolithic Jericho B (6500–5500 B.C.) were kin to the craftsmen of the Early Pottery Neolithic Jericho of stratum IX, who first made sun-dried and then kiln-baked pottery there, mixed with straw as a binder. Bricks too were manufactured in this fashion. In a much later age, Israelite slaves in Egypt were to find their burden unbearable when Pharaoh refused to give them straw for the bricks they were forced to provide for his building projects.

After the initial appearance of kiln-baked pottery in the first half of the fifth millennium B.C., pottery-making began to improve rapidly, changing sufficiently as each age passed by to enable it to become an index of history. By the Middle Bronze Age, spanning the first half of the second millennium B.C., it had achieved an excellence that in some respects was never to be surpassed in later Palestine.

There is a remarkable vase from Jericho belonging to the seventeenth century B.C. The potter turned on his wheel a graceful carinated, trumpet-foot vase typical of the period; then molding it by hand into the likeness of one of his contemporaries, he baked it into a monument to his memory that has endured now for thousands of years. The representation is highly stylized, but the exaggerated eyebrows, large round eyes incised after baking, nose protruding like a wedge-shaped blade from the forehead, full lips, spade beard, ears extended to form handles, hair on face and of beard indicated by pinholes—all these unmistakably portray a sharply intelligent, quizzically energetic Semite. The vase has been nicknamed "Jericho John" by irreverent archaeologists because of the supposed likeness to the late Professor John Garstang, who conducted important excavations at Jericho in the nineteen-twenties.

A glowing description of the fruitful oasis of Jericho is given by the first-century historian Josephus. "There is a fountain by Jericho, that runs plentifully. . . . The report is, that this fountain, at the beginning, caused not only the blasting of the earth and the trees, but of the children born of women, . . . but that it was made gentle, and very wholesome and fruitful, by the prophet Elisha. . . . It . . . passes along a plain . . . wherein it affords nourishment to those most excellent gardens that are thick set with trees. There are in it many sorts of palm trees that are watered by it, different from each other in taste and name. . . . This country withal produces honey from bees; it also bears that balsam which is the most precious of all the fruits in that place, cypress trees also. . . . He who should pronounce this place to be divine would not be mistaken. . . . It will not be easy to light on

183

any climate in the habitable earth that can well be compared to it." [1] The fertility of the plains of Jericho and Beth-shan has continued undiminished.

No wonder Joshua's troops and their families looked with eager eyes on this earthly paradise. They coveted it and they conquered it. And then the years were to run away like sand pouring out of an hourglass. In time Saul became king of Israel, only to fall in battle before the Philistines and have his body impaled on the wall of Beth-shan. David hung up his lyre, seized the scepter of kingship and ruled firmly with cunning and sometimes cold-blooded hand, though often racked with fiercer passions and fiercer griefs. Solomon succeeded him and raised Israel by his genius to a position of power and importance without parallel in its earlier or later history. Israel shone in Solomon's glory at the expense of having foisted upon it a despotic Oriental monarchy. The evil Solomon did lived after him; much of the good perished with his passing. His painfully built-up kingdom was split lastingly asunder after his death. Israel and Judah parted company, to succumb separately to foreign forces. Having wasted much of their strength in mutual enmity, they were easily overrun, Israel by Assyria toward the end of the eighth century B.C. and Judah by Babylonia near the beginning of the sixth.

The turn of the wheel

Look back in imagination nearly twenty-five hundred years to the time of King Zedekiah at the mob fleeing in wild disorder along the road from Jerusalem to Jericho. This was the army of the king of Judah, worsted in battle against the Babylonians, looking for an escape from the inevitable. Zedekiah had raised his hand in reckless rebellion against Babylon, and now he was a fugitive from Jerusalem. He had ruled there merely by sufferance, for Babylon had already established its power over Palestine. In a move of desperation he had sought to rule not as a puppet but in freedom and by right, as others had before him. He had gambled and lost. Now to escape, if possible, to the hills on the east side of the Jordan, or farther even into the reaches of the desert, whence the Bene-Israel had once emerged.

But escape was not to be. The Judaeans had almost reached the green

[1] Josephus, *War*, IV, 8, 3.

gardens of Jericho, where they had hoped to find at least a brief respite, when the pursuing Babylonian troops overtook them. Among the prisoners taken were Zedekiah and the young princes, who were carried to the camp of Nebuchadnezzar. Cruel vengeance was to be exacted. The Chaldean monarch would now make it absolutely clear that he was indeed the master of Palestine and was not to be trifled with. He would have his pleasure of these captives. Executioners unsheathed their swords. A fire was kindled and iron rods were placed in it. A nod, and the stupefied children were slain in front of their father. All light went out of his face. What mattered it now that he was grasped tightly, while the glowing metal was pressed first against one eyeball and then against the other, scarring them sightless.

"Zedekiah rebelled against the king of Babylon.... Thereupon, Nebuchadnezzar king of Babylon came with all his army against Jerusalem, and laid siege to it, and they built siegeworks against it.... Then a breach was made in the city wall, and the king with all the men of war fled.... But the army of the Chaldeans pursued the king, and overtook him in the plains of Jericho.... They slew the sons of Zedekiah before his eyes, and put out the eyes of Zedekiah and bound him in fetters and took him to Babylon" (II Kings 24:20–25:1–7).

Thus ended the history of the first kingdom of Judah. The wheel had turned a full revolution. The path from Jericho to Jerusalem and back again had proved a short one. Joshua's people were again crossing the Jordan, but this time eastward into exile, to sing songs of loneliness by the rivers of Babylon. However, the soil of Palestine had entered into their innermost being, and they were never again able to sever themselves from it. "By the waters of Babylon, there we sat and wept when we remembered Zion.... If I forget you, O Jerusalem, let my right hand wither. Let my tongue cleave to the roof of my mouth, if I do not remember you, if I do not set Jerusalem above my highest joy" (Psalm 137:1–6).

God had walked abroad in the Promised Land and had made His voice heard. Prophets and priests and the lowliest shepherds had listened, and the message has remained imprinted in the hearts of commoners and kings. The waters of the Jordan thenceforth laved a land from which the Torah, the Teaching of the Lord and His Law, was continuously to go forth. Palestine became spiritually what the facts of geography had made it physically, the focal point of the world, with Jerusalem its central city and the Jordan the world's central stream.

Palestine's blessing and curse lies in its geographic position, which makes it a bridge between the nations. It is a crossroads on the deathless trade routes between East and West. Its strategic importance in more recent times has been recognized and fought over by Richard the Lion-hearted and Saladin, by Napoleon and Nelson, by Allenby and Liman von Sanders, by Wavell and Rommel. It stands between Asia and Africa, between Europe and Arabia, whose desert sands cover an ocean of oil. The miracle of modern Israel has now come into being, and the array of its enemies is indicative of its importance and creative progress.

With regard to Palestine the great geopolitical pathfinder, Halford J. Mackinder, wrote:

In a monkish map, contemporary with the Crusades, which still hangs in Hereford Cathedral, Jerusalem is marked as the geometrical center of the world, and on the floor of the Church of the Holy Sepulchre in Jerusalem they will show you till this day the precise spot which is the center. If our study of the geographical realities, as we now know them in completeness, is leading us to right conclusions, the medieval ecclesiastics were not far wrong. If the World-Island be inevitably the principal seat of humanity on this globe, and if Arabia, as the passage land from Europe to the Indies and from the Northern to the Southern Heartland, be central in the World-Island, then the hill-citadel of Jerusalem has a strategic position with regard to world realities not differing essentially from its ideal position in the perspective of the Middle Ages, or its strategical position between ancient Babylon and Egypt. . . .[2]

Change of guard

Before being banished in large numbers to Babylonia, the Judaeans had been rooted in Palestine for seven centuries. Many of those who had been torn from what had for so long been their ancestral home seized the very first opportunity to return. When their conquerors succumbed to the power of Persia, their new masters gave these early Zionists permission to go up again to the Promised Land. With the active assistance of kings Cyrus and Darius in the latter part of the sixth century B.C., and of Arta-xerxes I about the middle of the fifth, they made increasingly successful

[2] Halford J. Mackinder, *Democratic Ideals and Reality*, p. 89.

efforts to resettle in Judah, to rebuild the walls of Jerusalem, restore the Temple, and re-establish the community according to the theocratic concepts they had mulled over while in exile. Among "the citizens whom Nebuchadnezzar, king of Babylon, had carried captive to Babylonia, and [who] returned to Jerusalem and Judah, each to his own town" are listed 345 inhabitants of Jericho (Ezra 2:1, 34). How glad they must have been to see their city of palms again, how delighted their children born abroad must have been with it! There were changes, to be sure. Among the chief of them was the fact, to which they themselves were to contribute, that vernacular Hebrew was giving way to Aramaic. The Book of Ezra, which recorded their history, was composed partly in that dialect.

Change now followed change in Palestine and Transjordan, and naturally also in the Jordan Valley. After the Persians came the Greeks. And Greek influence was in many ways the most important and fateful ever to spread across the land. With method and persistence Alexander the Great (333–323 B.C.) and the generals who succeeded him carried out the Hellenization of most of the Near East. Greek influence spread as far south as Arabia and as far east as India. I have excavated black glazed Greek sherds of the last part of the fifth century B.C. at Ezion-geber (Elath) on the north shore of the east arm of the Red Sea. I have found at Khirbet Tannur in southern Transjordan a Nabataean altar bearing in Greek characters the composite Graeco-Semitic name of its donor, Alexandros Amrou. There too I have dug up Nabataean gods whose images were hardly distinguishable at first glance and in some respects from figures of Zeus, Atargatis, Helios and Tyche elsewhere in the Hellenistic world. These were the gods worshiped also in the Hellenistic-Roman temples in such places as Caesarea Philippi, Scythopolis (Beth-shan), Gadara, Pella, Gerasa and Philadelphia (Rabbath-Ammon). They were thus also well known throughout the Jordan Valley.

I have picked up a Rhodian jar handle on an ancient site in the Jordan Valley. It could be dated, by the name of a Greek eponym impressed on it, to the first part of the second century B.C. At that time the Greek-speaking garrisons and settlements scattered through Palestine and Transjordan preferred the resinated wine imported from the island of Rhodes to the local products. Hellenism was widespread northward from the magnificent metropolis of Alexandria, which for a long period was the greatest city in the world, and southward from the capital established by Seleucus at Antioch on the Orontes after the death of Alexander. Powerful streams of Greek cultural influence converged upon Palestine.

If Greeks came to Palestine, Jews returned the compliment and went abroad in great numbers, of their own free will. The Jewish community in Alexandria, living under the Ptolemaic dynasty that controlled Palestine from 301 to 198 B.C., became so large and so well-assimilated to its Greek environment that its members could no longer read the Bible in the original Hebrew. A Greek translation, the Septuagint, came into being, parts of it being completed by the middle of the third century B.C. Greek philosophy influenced some Jewish writings. The Jewish poet Philo wrote an epic poem on Jerusalem in Greek. Other Jewish documents, written originally in Aramaic or Hebrew, have been preserved only in Greek translations. For three centuries before and for centuries after the time of Christ, Greek cultural influence predominated in greater Palestine, manifesting itself steadily during the Roman and Byzantine periods. Nevertheless, the country remained Hebraic at core, stubbornly proud of its prophetic and priestly traditions.

This became apparent when Antiochus IV, known also as Antiochus Epiphanes, ascended the Syrian throne and made a violent attempt forcibly to Hellenize all of Judaea. He belonged to the Seleucid dynasty, established in Syria, that in 198 B.C. had replaced the Egyptian Ptolomies as the controlling power over Palestine. It became a fundamental part of his policy to turn the Jews away from their Lord, and to make them identify themselves completely with Greek culture in all its aspects. But Antiochus was to find the Jews a stiff-necked people, who persisted in worshiping in their own way regardless of consequences. So now he forbade circumcision and the observance of the Sabbath under penalty of death. He made pagan sacrifices obligatory on the part of the Jews and attempted to force them to eat swine's flesh. Not content with plundering the Temple of many of its finest treasures, he set up an altar dedicated to Olympian Zeus on the sacred altar of burnt offering in the Temple itself. This desecration occurred in 168 B.C., igniting a rebellion that had long been smoldering. Led by the Maccabees, a fitful freedom was achieved under the Hasmonaean dynasty, whose uneasy rule endured for little over a century, to be ended by Pompey. Then the government fell into the ruthlessly capable hands of Herod, known as the Great. This occurred shortly after the death of his

Idumaean father, Antipater, who had been the real power behind the throne of the last Maccabaean king, Hyrcanus II.

HEROD THE GREAT

Throughout his long reign, from 37 to 4 B.C., Herod the Great proved to be a champion of the Jews, a friend of the Romans and an admirer of the Greeks. In actual practice he was a dangerous despot who feared for his position and bore down with murderous hand upon every possible source of uprising. He even had three of his own sons executed. No wonder Augustus was to say of him that it was better to be Herod's pig than his son. However, he maintained peace in Palestine, and that was what his Roman masters, to whom it had become subject, demanded above all from the governors of their provinces. Of all his domain he loved best the valley of the Jordan.

Herod was no uncouth provincial, but a well-traveled and highly cultured man who lived in a strongly Hellenized part of the world under Roman dominion. He was a polished diplomat who knew to a nicety how to gain the respect and friendship of a succession of Roman rulers, from Caesar through Mark Antony and Augustus. Upon their favor depended his own weal and the welfare of his country and people. To each in turn Herod was wise enough to pay unwaveringly loyal fealty.

This cosmopolitan part-Jew, whose mother was Nabataean and whose father was of Idumaean extraction, was in effect one of the greatest ambassadors to the Gentiles the Jews had ever had. During his reign, as a result of his wise statesmanship, no foreign armies pillaged Palestine. He was one of the few who resisted the lures of the insatiable Cleopatra. She had already obtained parts of Arabia and the rich Jericho region as a gift from Mark Antony, who was as wax in her arms. Then she came to Jerusalem, scheming to trade her fleeting favors as the price of some of Herod's finest possessions. In him, however, she met her match. Indeed, Herod was disposed to have her killed, a move of advantage to Mark Anthony and himself, but his council of friends dissuaded him. At least this is the story that Josephus would have us believe. So "he treated Cleopatra kindly, and made her presents, and conducted her on her way to Egypt," after having "farmed of her parts of Arabia, and those revenues that came to her from the region about Jericho." [3]

[3] Josephus, *Antiquities*, XV, 4, 2.

So far as his general education and outlook are concerned, Herod was more Roman than Jew. Like Solomon, whom he resembled in some respects, Herod had a passion for building. The peace he brought his country endowed it with a great prosperity and secured for himself great riches, with which he embarked on a vast public-works program. He altered the aspect of Jerusalem, making it an imposing Graeco-Roman metropolis. His crowning achievement there, and for the people of the land his constant curse, was the construction of the third Temple. It was not completely finished till A.D. 63–64, many years after Herod's death. Six years later the Romans destroyed it, after crushing the Jewish rebellion against them, and it was never again rebuilt. Herod's House of God was in form largely a Greek temple, a fact heightened by the golden eagle he had set up above its great gate. When a premature report of his death was broadcast, the eagle was pulled down to the applause of the multitude. Josephus probably inferred correctly that the building of a new resplendent temple in Jerusalem by Herod stemmed less out of a sense of piety than from a desire to raise "an everlasting memorial" to himself. [4] Parts of the Herodian structure are still visible.

In another burst of public building, this time to help celebrate the quinquennial games instituted in almost all Roman provinces to commemorate the anniversary of the Battle of Actium, in which Caesar Augustus defeated the combined fleets of Antony and Cleopatra, Herod erected in Jerusalem a theater, an amphitheater and a hippodrome. He even established an endowment fund to pay for prizes and sacrifices at the Olympian games.

The magnificent edifices in Jerusalem represented, however, only a part of Herod's contribution to the architecture of Palestine. He built according to a master plan which made for the adornment, security and general well-being of the country. In the Jordan Valley alone he built a string of fortresses and towns stretching all the way from Jericho to Banias. "He also built a city . . . in the valley of Jericho, as you go from it northward, whereby he rendered the neighboring country more fruitful by the cultivation its inhabitants introduced; and this also he called Phasaelus," [5] in memory of his brother Phasaelus. To the north he had his youngest brother, Pheroras, rebuild the towering Hasmonaean fortress of Alexan-

[4] *Ibid.*, 11, 1.
[5] *Ibid.*, XVI, 5, 2.

drium (Qarn Sartabeh), which is located on top of a great hill commanding a view of much of the length of the Jordan Valley.

The city of Jericho, however, received Herod's special attention. He adorned it with a beautiful theater and a fine hippodrome. He also built there a citadel which he named Cypros, in honor of his mother, and a tower which he called Phasaelus after his brother. He also gave the name of Phasaelus to one of the towers of a fortress he erected in Jerusalem, near the present Jaffa gate, in addition to the Antonia palace he erected near the Temple area. He built Antipatris in honor of his father. Herod loved his relatives when they were dead.

The richness and warmth of the oasis of Jericho delighted Herod and soothed his nerves. Its remoteness from Jerusalem relieved his worries, for he was in constant fear, as every harsh dictator must be, for his personal safety. He spent his last days in Jericho, rotting away into a miserable death like an overripe melon in the hot sun.

From Jerusalem it was but a few hours' chariot ride southwestward to the powerful fortress of Herodium, which Herod the Great had built anew and named for himself. It looks from the air like an extinct volcano. Thence a direct track led down southeastward to the mighty, almost inaccessible bastion of Masada, overlooking the Dead Sea. He greatly strengthened this naturally strong fortress crag, making it virtually impregnable. Although Jerusalem was conquered by the Romans in A.D. 70, it took three years more before Masada succumbed to their massive siege in A.D. 73. Tremendous circumvallation walls to fence in all exits from and approaches to the fortress and starve out its defenders had been required before victory could be achieved. Even then it came not through frontal assault, but because the surviving remnant of the Judaean garrison, numbering 900, committed mass suicide rather than submit to Roman capture. In death they defeated their enemy who lusted to parade them in ignominy and as a dire warning to others at a triumphal homecoming in Rome.

Herod's rebuilding did not end here. He also renovated the fortress of Machaerus, towering over the northeast side of the Dead Sea. From the Mediterranean to beyond the Jordan, he established a number of powerful bastions, including a second Herodium near Mount Nebo, and also strengthened Hyrcanus, about 8 miles southeast of Jerusalem, seeking thus to secure himself from foreign enemies as well as from internal opposition and rebellion. Herod trusted neither Rome nor Jerusalem.

The great seaport and governmental center of Caesarea Maritima on the western coast and Sebaste (Sebastieh) on the hilltop site of the ruins of the Israelite capital city of Samaria further testified to his building mania and the wealth and magnificence marking his brilliant and brutal reign. Like Caesarea, Sebaste was named in honor of his patron, Caesar Augustus, whose Latin name was so rendered in Greek (from Sebastos).[6] Herod settled 6000 veterans there, including Greek mercenaries. Indeed he depended greatly upon his utterly reliable and completely ruthless mercenaries, including Germans, Greek Thracians and Galatians from Asia Minor. Their use helped embitter the populace against him, as did his reliance upon foreigners for some of the most important offices of his government. A Greek, Nicolaus of Damascus, with his brother Ptolemy, were among Herod's chief counselors, and another Ptolemy was his finance minister.

Herod scattered his largesse far and wide, both inside and outside his own country. The taxes imposed upon his people must have been exceedingly severe, to yield so much of the wealth he spent with calculated profligacy. His aim was to bolster his power and also to further his country's foreign trade, especially with Rome and her dependencies. He beautified Ascalon, where his vicious sister Salome, who exercised such a baleful influence upon him, lived.[7] Gaza too benefited from his generosity. In addition, Acre, Tyre, Sidon, Berytus, Antioch and Damascus in Phoenicia and Syria were recipients of buildings he donated. There were others even farther afield—in Rhodes, Chios, Nicopolis, Athens and Sparta. At Rhodes he paid for the building of a temple devoted to Pythian Apollo.

Herod was an immensely able and complex person, sometimes completely charming and at other times utterly abominable. He was an amazingly successful diplomat, a brilliant soldier, an admirable administrator, a cunning politician, violent lover, heartless father and in general an absolute and undependable autocrat within the broad limitations of Roman tolerance. He ruled with force, lived in frenzy and perished in frightening senility. One of his very last commands resulted in the execution of another of his sons, Antipater.

Herod was a child of his age. His code was that of the Caesars of Rome. He lived up to and in many respects surpassed the standards by which they measured success. Had he been born in other times and under different

---

[6] Dio Cassius, *Roman History*, LIII, XVI, 8.
[7] Josephus, *War*, II, 6, 3.

conditions, he might well have eclipsed the emperors to whom he paid allegiance. As it is, Josephus quotes Augustus and Agrippa as saying, "The dominions of Herod were too little for the greatness of his soul; for that he deserved to have both all the kingdom of Syria, and that of Egypt also." [8] His buildings, however, were soon shattered. His achievements hardly survived his death. For eight thousand years before him men had been building palaces in places like Jericho, only to have their work dissolve like the evening dew in the morning sun. Heaps of rubble, piles of great blocks, fragments of tremendous walls, a few outstanding ruins are all that remain here and there in Palestine and Transjordan of Herod's resplendent structures. As often as not, many of the remains of his great building enterprises are concealed under decrepit hovels and village dumps. But in his day and for some time thereafter Herod's harbor works and fortresses, his hippodromes and temples attested to the wealth and power he achieved for himself and his country.

It is not difficult to project one's self backward to a triumphal scene of Herod's career. Listen to the flourish of trumpets, the roll of drums, the clash of cymbals, the clatter of a cavalcade. Hurry, citizens and slaves, patricians and shepherds, Jews and Romans—run to see the stirring spectacle! Marcus Agrippa, the great marshal and diplomat, who was the Roman governor of Syria for ten years from 23 B.C., and who represented the Roman imperium with an authority only a little less than that of Caesar Augustus himself, has arrived! And with him Herod, radiant, resplendent. Truly, these two do not make the appearance of master and servent, but of monarchs of equal rank—the imperious Agrippa and the dynamic Herod. Look, they are walking now, arm in arm, both smiling and nodding graciously to the cheering throngs. Aye, clap hands, sound the joyous hallel, let song echo from wall to wall! Who can refrain from being swept away by the happy excitement, from forgetting his doubts about this pomp and pageantry in the cheer of the moment! "When Herod . . . understood that Marcus Agrippa had sailed again out of Italy into Asia, he made haste to him, and besought him to come . . . into his kingdom, and to partake of what he might justly expect from one that had been his guest and was his friend. . . . Agrippa agreed, and came into Judaea; whereupon Herod omitted nothing that might please him. . . . He . . . showed him . . . Sebaste

[8] Josephus, *Antiquities*, XVI, 5, 1.

and Caesarea . . . that port that he had built, and . . . the fortresses which he had erected at great expenses, Alexandrium and Herodium and Hyrcania. He also conducted him to the city Jerusalem, where all the people met him in their festival garments, and received him with acclamations."[9]

For days such as these, for the taste of this triumph, Herod had labored all his life. Who could fail to read Agrippa's countenance and see how amazed and pleased he was with Herod and his works, how apprecia-tive of the peace which kept the channels of imperial trade open, how delighted he was with this cultured king of the Jews who had brought Rome to Jerusalem.

What Agrippa could not be expected to know, and what Herod him-self was hardly aware of, was the inner life of the people of the land. In the last analysis, the multitudes of simple, pious folk and the spiritual authori-ties they recognized were little touched by the majestic façades Herod reared everywhere in the land. In spite of all the glitter of the Hellenistic world about them, they remained firm in their adherence to the simple faith of their fathers.

HILLEL

There was, for instance, the gentle Jew, Rabbi Hillel, who lived in Jeru-salem at the time of Herod. He was active from approximately 30 B.C. to A.D. 10, being the Nasi, prince of the Sanhedrin, and a recognized leader among his people. In him was embodied, more than in any other man of his day, the spirit of the finest prophetic traditions. He was an exalted expo-nent of purest Judaism, which flowered unsullied in an environment in which hedonistic Hellenism manifested itself so ostentatiously. Hillel was above all the great teacher, who preached and practiced the virtues of charity, humility and real piety. He was a gigantic influence among his fellow Jews in his own generation, setting an inspired example for all men.

How well he knew the foibles of men; how insistently he urged that they be judged charitably! "Judge not your neighbor until you are in his place," he said (Aboth II:4). A few years later Jesus was to say: "Judge not, that you be not judged. . . . And why do you see the speck that is in your brother's eye, but do not notice the log that is in your own eye?" (Matthew

---

[9] *Ibid.*, XVI, 2, 1.

7:1–3). When asked by a proselyte to teach him the Torah in the shortest possible form, Hillel replied: "What is unpleasant to yourself, that do not do to your neighbor. This is the whole law, all else is but its exposition" (Shabbath 31a). Thus he evinced his intensely practical and deeply understanding way of explaining to the ordinary man the simple meaning of the Biblical injunction to love your neighbor as yourself contained in Leviticus 19:18. Jesus shortly thereafter was to say: "So whatever you wish that men would do to you, do so to them, for this is [the meaning of] the law and the prophets" (Matthew 7:12). A rabbinical tradition relates that once when the sages were assembled at Jericho a heavenly voice was heard, saying: "Among those here present is one who would have deserved the Holy Spirit to rest upon him, if the age he lived in had been worthy of it. And all eyes turned toward Hillel" (Tosefta Sotah XIII:3).

JESUS

In the same prophetic tradition Jesus continued to teach and interpret the Torah. Few in his generation were more familiar with its basic principles and enduring significance than this young Rabbi or Teacher (John 1:38). He answered the lawyer's question as to how eternal life might be inherited by making him recall two Biblical passages, one from Deuteronomy 6:5, "You shall love the Lord your God with all your heart, and with all your soul, and with all your might," and the other, "You shall love . . . your neighbor as yourself" (Leviticus 19:18; cf. 19:34), which Hillel had quoted to the proselyte (Shabbat 31a; Luke 10:25–27). With a parable Jesus replied to the legalistic question as to the exact meaning of the word *neighbor* in the Lukan passage: A traveler on his way from Jerusalem to Jericho fell among thieves. A priest and a Levite passed him by, heedless of his hurt. Finally, a certain Samaritan succored him, and lodged him in a neighboring inn at his own expense. The parable was ended. Was the point clear? "Which of these three," Jesus questioned his questioner, "proved neighbor to the man who fell among the robbers? And he [the lawyer] said, The one who showed him mercy. And Jesus said to him, Go and do likewise" (Luke 10:36, 37).

How gay are the crowds that throng the roads leading southward through the Jordan Valley to Jericho! The people are happy. The land is green. Newborn lambs and goats skip and frolic. The planted fields, beribboned with irrigation streams, are bursting with fullness. Waves of color mark ripples of motion as heavy heads of grain bow before the press of the winds. Swallows and brilliantly hued bee-eaters swoop about. Sweet smells fill the air. Lilting songs herald the coming of the happy pilgrims. The time of Passover is almost at hand, and all who are able are hastening to Jerusalem, to break the unleavened wafer at festival supper there. Each community along the entire length of the Jordan Valley, and from beyond Jordan too, has sent a delegation. They are making their joyful way to the mountain shrine of the City of Peace, to give thank-offerings for the first-fruits of the season and for the freedom from bondage anciently obtained by their ancestors. A natural halting place was always at fabulous Jericho, the valley gateway to the hilltop capital. Among the pilgrims is Jesus, who is to become known as the Prince of Peace. His offering is to be a supreme one, the sacrifice of his life.

Rome ruled Palestine not only through its Pontius Pilates, but also through a small minority of royalist Jews. These fought among themselves for the fat crumbs of position and privilege their masters threw them. Like their rulers, they resented and feared change, abhorred criticism and reproach. The like of these Romans and their puppets manifests itself in every generation and in every land. They had sneered at Amos in the high place at Bethel. They had thrust Jeremiah into prison in Jerusalem and subjected him throughout his life to such indignities that he cursed the day he was born. Listen to the jackals howling for his life when Jeremiah ventured to preach the word of God to his people, saying: "Thus says the Lord: If you will not listen to me, to walk in my law, . . . I will make this house like Shiloh, and . . . this city a curse for all the nations of the earth. . . . Then priests and the [professional] prophets cried out to the princes and to all the people, saying, 'This man deserves death' " (Jeremiah 26:4–6, 11). And of Jesus, too, their like said later: "He deserves death" (Matthew 26:66). And so Jesus was crucified, even as many other Jews, accounted dangerous to the regime, were crucified in his day.

From splendid Caesarea Philippi at the Banias source of the Jordan, Jesus had journeyed to Capernaum by the Sea of Galilee, where he preached in the synagogue. Thence he went to Judaea and crossed over to Jordan. Finally, he found his way back to the west side of the Jordan Valley, a few days before Passover, at Jericho, which Herod the Great had transformed into the likeness of a magnificent Roman city. And Jesus, perforce aware of the splendor of the palaces and the power of the princes in

Jericho, must have reflected how pitiful and puny and transitory all this arrogant grandeur really was. He must already have entertained the thought to which, shortly afterward, he gave concrete expression in Jerusalem when he said, "Render therefore to Caesar the things that are Caesar's; and to God the things that are God's" (Matthew 22:21). It was with kindly graciousness, therefore, that he could take lodging overnight at Jericho in the elegant house of the rich little tax collector Zacchaeus, whom he inspired to make adequate restitution for moneys unrightfully acquired, and, in addition, to make a large capital gift to the poor (Luke 19:1–10). Zacchaeus achieved thus greater fame through his chance charity than he could possibly have gained otherwise. His entire being had become illumined by coming into contact, however briefly, with a spiritual flame. By prescient faith was the blind man Bartimaeus healed, when he met Jesus in Jericho (Mark 10:51). A monastery nests on a mountaintop by Jericho, founded in the belief that it marks the spot where Jesus resisted the temptation after his baptism (Matthew 4:7–11).

VIII / The Plains of Moab

Teleilat Ghassul

Every motion of the artist's brush was followed with rapt attention by the gaping audience. Divinity, strange and striking, was coming to life in the wall-painting. And now the finishing touches were being put to this great fresco, fairly aflame with the hues of the rainbow. Beginning at the left, a large sun cast its blaze upon a nude god, with seven attendant deities beyond him. In brilliant red and yellow, in startling black and white, these fateful figures were assuming final form. They covered a lime-surfaced, mud-brick wall 13 feet long. Already complete was one painting showing a great multicolored eight-pointed star radiantly surrounded by a galaxy of gods fearful to behold, foreign to a mortal world. There was also a many-hued painting of a fearsome mask such as perhaps the chief priest wore. On yet another wall, in sharp contrast of style, was a painting of a bird, vibrantly alert, achieving such naturalistic effect that long ages must elapse before its artistic excellence could again be attained.

The brush is still, the artist has stepped back. Overcome by the immensity of his portrayal, he bows his head and intones a prayer. The onlookers join in. The painter is one of their priests, the walls enclose their shrine, the paintings trace the pattern of their belief in the supernatural.

The faith of these people is firm, the forms of their religion sometimes frightful. A procession is approaching the shrine with singing and wailing, with ecstatic dancing and declaiming. What objects are those carried in its van? A large empty pottery jar, and in the hands of another bearer an infant! Is it silent in slumber or stilled in death? The procession halts in front of the shrine. The priests emerge, the ceremony commences, the child's body is inserted into this strange receptacle and the jar is sealed. From whose lips escaped that strangled moan? Such was the gift to the gods of fertility that the earth might yield its riches, the herds bountifully produce their young, the women bear sons in plenty. Their sacrifice would serve as a foundation offering. Surely the house reared over it would enjoy the favor of the divine! See how the gods painted on the walls gleam with satisfaction. To them the fruit of the womb that the womb may again become fruitful!

Would you like to visit this shrine and gaze at these deities? It is located in a bustling town of considerable size which stands among green fields in the partly irrigated plain at the northeast end of the Dead Sea. Pay the boatmen a fraction of the whole shekel he demands for his services and have yourself put across the Jordan, whose flood is surging toward the Dead Sea now clearly in sight. If you have told him your goal, he will set you ashore on the east side of the river at a point about 4½ miles north of its outlet into the Sea. You will have to go about 3 miles straight east to reach your destination. There is a salt-encrusted waste to traverse, then up some serried slopes of barren earth where rarely a blade of grass grows, before you get to the top of the plain. And then you will have to be nimble, because every so often you will have to jump across an irrigation ditch several feet broad, whose waters come from the Brook Heshbon (Wadi Hesban). Everywhere you look there seems to be a thriving settlement whose carefully cultivated fields stretch east all the way to the base of the Mountains of Moab. You are in the Plains or Fields of Moab.

But you have waited too long! The site you proposed to visit no longer exists, except as an almost unrecognizable ruin, so razed by men and ravished by time that it is barely distinguishable from the uncultivated waste in which it is now set. It is known today as Teleilat Ghassul. Look about you! There are still some irrigated patches in the plain, but no villages, practically no life. To the Jesuit Fathers Alexis Mallon and Robert Koeppel, who discovered and excavated this site, followed thirty years later by Father Robert North, we owe our present information about it. The ruins of four towns were revealed through their labors, and rescued thus from the oblivion into which they had fallen. First established early in the fourth millennium B.C., in the Chalcolithic or Copper-and-Stone period, the story of the settlements which superseded one another there can be followed by means of their physical remains for about four hundred years, until the end of that particular civilization.

In addition to hand-made pottery and worked flints, copper ornaments, tools and weapons were employed at Teleilat Ghassul. They have been found in other Chalcolithic sites too, such as Tell Abu Matar, Bir es-Safadi and Khirbet el-Beytar by Beersheba. Some of the Chalcolithic copper implements of both secular and sacred nature found in one of the Nahal Hever caves in the hills above Ain Gedi on the west side of the Dead Sea were magnificent creations, indicative of high metallurgical and artistic skills.

Fragments of fascinating frescoes, almost modernistic in style, painted on lime surfaces were discovered on the inner side of some of the sun-baked, mud-brick walls of rectangular houses in the next-to-last (third) city at Teleilat Ghassul. Some of the walls had received four or five coats of paint, a new one, apparently, being applied when the preceding one had flaked off, or when an impelling religious impulse animated the artist or his patron. Only the fresco with the painting of the lifelike bird had remained comparatively intact when the excavators opened the site. The others were all in greater or less ruin owing to the collapse of all or parts of the walls on which they were painted. Numerous fragments of dramatic paintings of birds were found, one depicted with primitive forcefulness. The exact nature of these gods, portrayed and worshiped more than 5500 years ago, and the character of the religion built up around them remain more or less an enigma. The main finds, however, indicate a primitive fertility cult.

Thousands of years ago, irrigation agriculture was practiced in the Plains of Moab and throughout most of the Jordan Valley. That requires considerable skill, long experience, an advanced degree of civilization. Men had to organize for their mutual welfare. The equitable use of available water had to be decided in communal council. In general, the lowlands of the Jordan Valley, including the Plains of Moab, seem to have been inhabited many hundreds of years, even millennia, before the rugged, heavily wooded hill country of Transjordan and Cisjordan was partly cleared and settled. To be sure, a site like Beida, located at a strategic point on a main travel route in the highlands of Transjordan at a point about 5 miles north of Petra, was settled as early as the first part of the seventh millennium B.C., partially contemporary with Pre-Pottery Neolithic Jericho A. And when, later on, after settlements had sprung up in numerous places in the hill country, and, on occasion, famine would occur because of lack of rain, there would be a movement to the lowlands, where perennial streams and the possibilities of irrigation made the peasants more independent of the vagaries of weather. "Now it came to pass, in the days when the Judges ruled, that there was a famine in the land. And a certain man of Beth-lehem-judah went to sojourn in the fields of Moab" (Ruth 1:1).

And so the inhabitants of Teleilat Ghassul planted and harvested, stored their surplus grain in moistureproof clay bins, built houses and shrines and developed through painful process of experiment the arts of civilization. To be sure, although they utilized hand-made, kiln-baked pottery and made excellent flint and fine copper tools, they never achieved some of the heights of civilization evinced in moats, city walls and towers that were attained by the much earlier inhabitants of Pre-Pottery Jericho. Many of their utensils were of stone. Mortars, pestles, loom weights, rub-bing stones abound—and they spell endless motions of daily toil. Grain had to be ground, skins cleaned and a host of duties performed. Their hand-made, well-fired and long-enduring pottery was of such a distinctive kind that even fragments of it can be recognized by the expert and spell out a long period of occupation by village-dwellers who used much the same Chalcolithic wares as are found elsewhere in Palestine and Transjordan.

Such were the household goods at Teleilat Ghassul—simple, plain, penurious by some standards but sufficient for their needs. A man fashioned a house by making mud bricks of rounded or flattened form with his hands and laying them in place after they had dried in the sun. The women plas-tered the walls inside and out with a coating of mud, and repaired the flat roofs every year or two. Under the thresholds of some of the houses, chil-dren were buried in pottery jars. Were such homes not indeed temples? Stone-lined graves were found where the dead were buried with ornaments and pottery vessels which probably contained food for them in the after-world. The concern of men with life after death is an extremely ancient one.

And then, sometime early in the second half of the fourth millennium B.C., Teleilat Ghassul was destroyed—by whom we do not know. It was never rebuilt. It is probably safe to assume that it was destroyed during some Bedouin raid. Scornful of agriculture, contemptuous of sedentary life, loathing houses and loving their airy and easily movable tents, content with little, bound down by few possessions, the nomads are ever on the alert for an opportunity to break down what they themselves will not build, to purloin the grain cultivated by the painful labor of others, to reduce planted fields to unplowed grazing lands, to pitch their tents on mounds which, unknown to them, mark the ruins of former towns.

Balaam's ass

I have met many Arabs in the Jordan Valley and in the Plains of Moab who, it seemed to me, were but a step in distance and a moment in time removed from figures familiar from the pages of the Bible. Such a one was Abdul Selim, who accompanied me on my visit to Teleilat Ghassul and elsewhere in the Plains of Moab. He was the headman of the small collection of mud-brick houses called Khirbet Sweimeh, located in the Plains of Moab at the northeast end of the Dead Sea. Its name resembles that of the nearby Biblical site of Beth-jeshimoth. Abdul Selim looked the part of a Biblical character. Tall and lean, serene and dignified, by repute fierce in wrath but just and honest after his fashion, it was obvious that he was a person of parts, however poor his mantle and empty his purse. I could not help telling him the story of Balak, king of Moab, and of Balaam, the soothsayer from Aram, whom Balak had importuned to curse the Bene-Israel encamped in these very Plains of Moab, on the east side of the Jordan, opposite the Plain of Jericho. He was fascinated by the account. "And the Bene-Israel set out and encamped in the Plains of Moab, beyond the Jordan, at Jericho. And Balak the son of Zippor saw all that Israel had done to the Amorites. And Moab was in great dread of the people because they were many. . . . So Balak . . . who was king of Moab at that time, sent messengers to Balaam the son of Beor . . . to call him, saying . . . come now . . . curse this people" (Numbers 22:1–6).

Abdul Selim listened intently and kept on asking if indeed this were written in Sacred Writ. When I went on to tell him how, despite the offer of king's ransom, Balaam refused to curse, but in accordance with God's command uttered words of blessing instead, he nodded his head in complete approval. And when in this connection I told him the story of Bala-am's ass, I had to pull out my little pocket Bible and translate for him, amid numerous "Ya Allah's" and "Allahu akbar's" on his part, the fascinating tale of the wise little beast. We practically wept together over the way Balaam beat his ass three times because she refused to go forward, seeing what Ba-laam could not see—that the angel of the Lord with drawn sword in hand barred the way. "Then the Lord opened the mouth of the ass and she said unto Balaam, . . . Am I not your ass, upon which you have ridden all your life long to this day? Have I ever been in the habit of making a mockery of you? And he said, No. Then the Lord opened the eyes of Balaam, and he saw the angel of the Lord standing in the way, with his sword in his hand: and he bowed his head, and fell on his face. And the angel of the Lord said unto him, Why have you struck your ass these three times? . . . If she had not turned aside from me, surely just now I would have slain you, and let her live. And Balaam said unto the angel of the Lord, I have sinned, for I did not know that it was you who were blocking the road against me" (Numbers 22:28, 30–34).

We had almost reached Abdul Selim's little village by that time. And there, standing stubbornly in the little narrow lane leading to it, was an obdurate donkey, heedless of its rider's blows, refusing to go forward. I, at least, and I think Abdul Selim too, looked hard up the lane, half expecting to see the angel of the Lord barring the way with his sword drawn in his hand.

Biblical sites

The name of Beth-jeshimoth, when transferred to the new site in the plain, became known as Bezemoth, written in some sources as Bethsimuth or Isimuth. Khirbet Sweimeh is its modern Arabicized version, but it cannot possibly be identified as the site of the original Beth-jeshimoth, because there is no pottery on its surface earlier than Hellenistic-Roman. The Bib-lical site is to be identified instead with the nearby elevated site of Tell el Azeimeh that overlooks a powerful spring. Similarly, in another instance, the Hellenistic-Roman and later Byzantine and medieval Arabic settle-ment, called in Greek and Talmudic sources Beth-nambris and Nimri and called today Tell Nimrin, got its name from the Biblical hill fortress of Beth-nimrah (called today Tell Bleibil), about a mile farther east and abandoned long before the new town was established.

Sometimes this transfer of names from one site to another in the Plains of Moab was complicated by the introduction of a completely foreign one. This occurred in the case of Tell er-Rameh, which is a conical, ruin-covered hill, located in the south-central part of the Plains of Moab. On and around it in Hellenistic-Roman times a new settlement was established over the ruins of an Iron Age Moabite site. The Hellenistic town was called Beth-aramphtha or Beth-ramtha, reflecting the Biblical name of Beth-haram, which had come to it, we believe, from the previously occupied hill fortress several miles away (now called Tell Iktanu), close to the eastern foothills of the Mountains of Moab. In 4 B.C. it was burned down. Herod Antipas rebuilt it on the lavish scale to which the Herodians were accustomed, and then gave it the completely new name of Livias, in honor of Augustus' wife. Subsequently the name was changed to Julias, when, on Augustus' death, Livia was adopted into the Julian *gens* and henceforth assumed the name of Julia Augusta. By that time, however, the name of Livias had taken root, and it survived till the sixth century A.D. Nevertheless, the more ancient name never died out among the native Aramaic-speaking population. When, finally, the comparatively new name of Livias fell into disuse, the old name of Beth-aramphtha or Beth-ramtha reappeared, as indicated by the present Arabic name of the site, Tell er-Rameh.

The possibility exists, of course, that Tell er-Rameh actually is the original Biblical site, but experience has taught us that the fortresses of that period were preferably located in the highlands above the plains, guarding the waters of springs or streams in their wadis as they emerged from the hills.

In another instance, both the original Biblical name of Abel-shittim and that of Roman-period Abila, derived from it and applied elsewhere, were forgotten. We believe that the Biblical site of Abel-shittim is to be identified with the nearby imposing mound of Tell el-Hammam in the once-forested hills of the Mountains of Moab. It has been possible by means of archaeological finds and literary materials to identify Abila with Khirbet Kefrein on the north side of the perennial stream of the Wadi Kefrein, but no trace whatsoever of the name Abila remains today in the Plains of Moab. Indeed, there is not a single place in the Plains of Moab where the Biblical name still remains in original or even in slightly Arabicized form as it does in other parts of the Jordan Valley at such places as Damieh, Eriha and Beisan (Adam or Adamah, Jericho and Beth-shan.)

John the Baptist

The irrigated and intensively cultivated Plains of Moab formed the fairest part of the province of Peraea. With Galilee, it had fallen to the inheritance of Herod Antipas in accordance with Herod the Great's last testament, in which he divided his kingdom among his three surviving sons. This was only one of the many times when the lands immediately east and west of the Jordan have been more or less arbitrarily partitioned. Abila and Livias (Julias, Beth-aramphtha) were the seats of the southernmost subsections or toparchies of Peraea. In the time of Herod the Great, the toparchy of Livias comprised eighteen villages. These toparchies of Livias and Abila were to be given later by Nero to Herod Agrippa II, the great-grandson of Herod the Great, having been previously annexed by Rome along with the rest of the kingdom of his father, Herod Agrippa I, after the latter's death.

In Herod Antipas' day the territory of Peraea stretched along the north half of the east side of the Dead Sea and along the east side of the Jordan River as far as the boundaries of Pella. In other words, it extended between the Arnon, Jabbok, and Jabesh (Wadi Yabis) rivers and somewhat beyond, taking in the lowlands and part of the hill country to the east of most of the Jordan River Valley. Machaerus was the southernmost fortress town of Peraea.

After the Romans, in A.D. 70, had finally crushed the hopeless Jewish rebellion against them, they destroyed Machaerus, as well as Herodium near Bethlehem, and in 73 captured the greatest fortress of all, Masada, overlooking the southwest shore of the Dead Sea. I have walked among the ruins of Machaerus, lost in wonder at the size of the site, and have marveled how its water supplies were secured through reservoirs and cisterns. Once it was a seat of power, short-lived in the record of history. It is remembered chiefly as the place where John the Baptist's head was struck off. Hellenized Jews who worshiped the Lord after a fashion and Hellenized Nabataeans who worshiped a whole pantheon of Graeco-Semitic fertility deities mingled there, among many other places, with proud Romans, to whom both were subject. None of them, however, could lastingly cope with the spiritual strength of Jews like John, whose power came from belief in God.

I have picked up numerous fragments of fine Roman and Nabataean pottery at Machaerus, where, according to the New Testament, Salome, at the instance of her mother Herodias, solicited and received the unkempt head of John the Baptist (Matthew 14:3–11). An Arab shepherd stood beside me as I held these sherds in my hands. In answer to his questions, I attempted to explain to him that through them I could read the history of a past to which both of us belonged. "And what do they say of the future?" he asked in utter simplicity. And I replied, "Allah yaref" (only God knows that).

John lived and died for the righteousness of the moral law. Prophetically intolerant of immorality, he was nevertheless possessed of the meekness that characterizes the immortals. Then Jesus came "from Galilee to the Jordan to John, to be baptized of him. John would have prevented him, saying, I have need to be baptized by you, and do you come to me? But Jesus answered him and said to him, let it be so now; for thus it is fitting for us to fulfill all righteousness" (Matthew 3:13–15). This son of the priest Zecharias (Luke 1:5, 57–63) had done no evil. He had preached the coming of the Kingdom of God. He had urged all who would listen to repent of their sins. He had washed penitents with the waters of the River Jordan in token of their change of heart. "In those days came John the Baptist, preaching in the wilderness of Judaea, Repent: for the kingdom of heaven is at hand. For this is he who was spoken of by the prophet Isaiah when he said, The voice of one crying in the wilderness: Prepare the way of the Lord, make his paths straight. . . . Then went out to him Jerusalem and all Judaea, and all the region about the Jordan, . . . confessing their sins" (Matthew 3:1–3, 5, 6).

But those entrenched in authority and power suspected that these simple religious teachings had revolutionary implications. So let this rabbi (John 3:26) be beheaded by a Herodian governing with the authority of Rome, and later on, let another rabbi, Akiba, be tortured to death by order of a representative of the same power for not yielding the right to proclaim and propagate the law of the Lord.

The Jordan was central in the life of John, as it was in the life of Jesus, whom he baptized in its waters, and in the life of Elijah with whom both of them were spiritually linked. To the Jordan all three of them repaired at important crises in their lives, seeking solace and inspiration by its banks and in the wastelands nearby. John, with "his garment of camel's hair, and a leathern girdle around his waist, . . . [whose] food was locusts and wild honey" (Matthew 3:4), looked and lived very much as Elijah had, especially during the latter's sojourn in the remote stretches of the Brook Cherith. Indeed, in the popular mind, Elijah, John, and Jesus were frequently confused. When the activities of Jesus were reported, Herod Antipas "was perplexed, because it was said by some that John had been raised from the dead; . . . but who is this, about whom I hear such things? And he sought to see him" (Luke 9:7–9). It remained for Pontius Pilate to be forever pilloried by ordering the crucifixion of Jesus.

It was meet that John should have labored beyond Jordan at Bethabarah (John 1:28) and lived in the land of Peraea, and that Jesus should have sojourned there too (John 1:28; Matthew 19:1; Mark 10:1; John 3:26, 10:40) because this was a Jewish land. So much so, in fact, that when the Jews of Galilee wanted to make the pilgrimage to Jerusalem to celebrate the Passover or other festivals, they chose to take the long roundabout trip through Peraea rather than the direct route through pagan and inhospitable Samaria. Had not Jesus, coming from Galilee, when once "he set his face to go [by the most direct and shortest route through Samaria] to Jerusalem" (Luke 9:51–53) been churlishly treated there? The Galileans would ford the Jordan, either near Scythopolis (Beisan) or farther downstream, journey southward along the east side of the Jordan Valley through Peraea to the Plains of Moab, reford the Jordan near its southern end, crossing over westward to Jericho, halt there for a while, and then continue to Jerusalem. Was not this the very journey that Jesus undertook?

It was while he was beyond Jordan that the rich young man had addressed him: "Teacher, what good deed must I do to have eternal life?" And Jesus had replied: "Why do you ask me about what is good? One there is who is good. If you would enter life, keep the Commandments. He said to him, Which? And Jesus said, You shall not kill, you shall not commit adultery, you shall not steal, you shall not bear false witness, honor your father and your mother, and you shall love your neighbor as yourself. The young man said to him, All these I have observed. What do I still lack? Jesus said to him, If you would be perfect, go, sell what you possess, and give it to the poor, and you will have treasure in heaven: and come, follow me. When the young man heard this, he went away sorrowful, for he had great possessions. Then said Jesus to his disciples, Truly I say to you, it will be hard for a rich man to enter the kingdom of heaven. Again I tell you, it is easier for a camel to go through the eye of a needle, than for a rich man to enter the kingdom of God" (Matthew 19:1, 16–24).

Jesus and John found ready audiences among the people of Peraea to whom they could preach. The hard core of the common folk there adhered firmly to the faith of their fathers, though many others were attracted to the Hellenistic-Roman way of life with which they came in constant contact. Theirs was in considerable part a rich land which, together with Galilee, yielded an income of two hundred talents a year to Herod Antipas, whose tetrarchy consisted of Galilee and Peraea. On the whole, they were well governed, even if despotically and at times harshly. In their spiritual life, however, they were directed by their rabbis and not by their rulers, and the masses distinguished sharply between their king and their God.

Herod Antipas

Herod Antipas, usually called Herod in the Gospels and correctly titled Herod the tetrarch in Matthew 14:1 and Luke 9:7, ruled Galilee and Peraea for forty-two years, from 4 B.C., the year of the death of his father, Herod the Great, to A.D. 39, when he was banished from his dominions by Caligula. What manner of man was this who exercised supreme power of life and death in these two provinces of Galilee and Peraea during the entire life span of Jesus and John?

Primarily it may be said of him that he was a Herodian. They formed a strange and capable family, these Herodians who were often more Roman than the Romans, both by necessity and to some degree by choice. Their life stories were swayed more by the stream of the Tiber than by the current of the Jordan, beside which they erected so many imposing edifices. Their aim, which they accomplished with brilliant if sycophantic success, was ever to please the Caesars they served. When they founded or rebuilt a city or fortress, they often named it after the reigning emperor or a member of his family. Herod Antipas was no exception. He founded a city on the shore of the Sea of Galilee and called it Tiberias after the stepson and successor of Augustus; he rebuilt Beth-aramphtha in the center of the Plains of Moab and renamed it Livias in honor of Augustus' queen, the mother of Tiberius. His half-brother, Herod Philip, had rebuilt Bethsaida on the north shore of the Sea of Galilee and renamed it Julias in honor of Augustus' daughter Julia. He had also enlarged and beautified Paneas at the easternmost source of the Jordan and renamed it Caesarea in honor of Augustus. Both Herod Philip and Herod Antipas, like their father, Herod the Great, were ardent builders of beautiful cities of Hellenistic architecture.

Herod Antipas was well aware of the fact that he administered his tetrarchy by sufferance of Rome and that his hold on his dominions hung by the fragile thread of imperial favor, despite the general excellence of his internal rule. He therefore took great pains to cultivate the friendship of his imperial patrons, and for that purpose journeyed frequently to Rome. During one of his visits there he became enamored of Herodias, the wife of his half-brother (also known to history as Herod), an exceptionally unambitious Herodian who was content to live at ease in Rome, far from the maddening politics of Palestine. That attachment was eventually to prove Antipas' undoing. It resulted immediately in arousing the enmity of his Nabataean neighbor and father-in-law, Aretas IV, whose daughter fled to Machaerus at the southern tip of Peraea overlooking the north end of the Dead Sea and then escaped to safety in Petra after discovering Herod Antipas' plans to divorce her in order to marry Herodias. Parenthetically it may be stated that this Herod who lived in Rome, and whose name may also have been Philip (Mark 6:17; Matthew 14:3), is not to be confused with the Herod Philip who built Caesarea Philippi and Julias (Bethsaida). They had different mothers.

Herodias, as her name indicates, was also a Herodian, and as passionate in the pursuit of her desires as any of her able and unscrupulous relatives. Her first husband, Herod (Philip), was her half-uncle; by a curious coincidence, so was her second, Herod Antipas. We are told that because of her fury, aroused by the rabbi's rebuke of her shameless remarriage—an abomination according to Jewish Law, which forbids a man to marry his brother's wife during his brother's lifetime (Leviticus 18:16)—John the Baptist was beheaded. Because of her insatiable appetite for pomp and power, Herod Antipas lost his position. His ignominious downfall was the direct result of her unceasing importunities that he beseech the emperor in Rome for rank higher than tetrarch, to match that of king given to her full brother, Herod Agrippa I. Herod Agrippa had been crowned king by Gaius Caesar, known as Caligula, over the tetrarchy of Batanaea and Trachonitis, which had previously belonged to his uncle, Herod Philip, and which included the cities of Caesarea Philippi and Julias (Bethsaida).

It mattered little to Herodias that her husband's tetrarchy of Galilee and Peraea was more important and yielded twice the income, although smaller in size than the one her brother had inherited. It galled her into a frenzy of jealously that her brother should be a king while she had to remain the spouse of a lower-ranking tetrarch. She was determined that her husband too must have a royal diadem placed upon his head, so that she might appear in public as a queen. So she nagged at Herod Antipas until he went to Rome to beg for a scepter. Herod Agrippa I, however, advised of his intentions and not minded to be outranked by his uncle, even though that uncle had befriended him when he was penniless and without position, managed to reach Caligula's ear first and implant a false accusation of treason. Herod Antipas was stripped of all authority and banished to Lyons in Gaul, where, be it said to her credit, Herodias voluntarily joined him in exile. At least we like to think that it was voluntary on her part. Herod Agrippa I thereupon fell heir to Herod Antipas' lands, and gradually succeeded in extending his authority all over the area once ruled by his grandfather, Herod the Great. Herod Antipas, tetrarch of Galilee and Peraea, the ablest of Herod the Great's sons, was thus swallowed up in oblivion, but still present in the hearts and minds of men are the teachings of John, whom he killed, and Jesus, whom he sought to see.

Journey's end

Like the frame of a harp, the Mountains of Moab enfold the Plains of Moab below them. Protectingly, the hills move forward till they frown down directly upon the Dead Sea. We sat on a height, Abdul Selim and I, with our backs against one of the numerous prehistoric dolmens in the vicinity, and gazed at the watered region extending between the mountains to the east and the river to the west, while I talked about the civilizations that had risen there. Only a few green patches of cultivation showed, although often in the past every acre had been employed. In these lowlands of the Plains of Moab, Joshua and Moses, John and Jesus, and many others before them had tarried and left their impress on their time, each man in his own way, each generation after its own fashion. And countless others had watched, as we were watching, the line of the Jordan wending its way to its appointed end.

I thought of Moses standing alone on nearby Mount Nebo, surveying this scene and looking long at the Promised Land on the west side of the Jordan, which he was fated never to cross. "And Moses went up from the Plains of Moab to Mount Nebo, to the top of Pisgah, which is opposite Jericho. And the Lord showed him all the land . . . and the Lord said to him, This is the land, of which I swore to Abraham, to Isaac and to Jacob, saying, I will give it to your descendants. I have let you see it with your eyes, but you shall not go over there. So Moses the servant of the Lord died there in the land of Moab according to the word of the Lord . . ." (Deuteronomy 34:1–5).

The Jungle of the Jordan is at its widest near the crossing before Jericho. Waves of heat make the misshapen grayish marl hills bordering it seem to dance a witch's waltz. The glint of the sea and the glare of the bare rock blind the eye. Fantastic rock formations stretch like an evil bar before the green oasis of Jericho, visible beyond them on a higher level. Above the gardens of this "City of Palms" soar the severe mountains of Judah, crowned faintly in the distance by the towers of Jerusalem.

All this, and more too, is what Moses "the man of God" (Psalms 90:1) saw as he stood alone on the summit of the mountain—alone, except for the companionship and call of the God he had never forsaken, and silent before this manifestation of another of the Lord's miracles. At last, the realization of a generation's striving, the accomplishment of an agony of effort, the fulfillment of driving dreams for freedom! But not for you, O Moses. Your work is done. For you, this is journey's end. The stream of your life is entering into the sea of death.

See how the Jordan builds for itself a curving delta to prolong for yet a forlorn while the length of its course. There! Its race is run. The life-giving river has reached and lost itself in the lifeless flood of the Dead Sea.

Swing low, sweet chariot,
Comin' for to carry me home;
I look'd over Jordan,
And what did I see,
Comin' for to carry me home,
A band of angels, comin' after me,
Comin' for to carry me home.

Chronology

PALAEOLITHIC AGE   Hunting and food gathering

LOWER   before 70,000 B.C.
  Pebble tools
  Bifacial tools
  Tabunian (or Tayacian) flaked tools

MIDDLE (MOUSTERIAN)   before 35,000 B.C.

UPPER   before 10,000 B.C.

NATUFIAN AGE (MESOLITHIC)   Cereal production, domestication of animals before 7000 B.C.

LOWER

UPPER

NEOLITHIC AGE   Villages, pottery

PRE-POTTERY   ca. 7000–5000 B.C.
  Jericho A (and Beida)   ca. 7000–6500 B.C.
  Jericho B   ca. 6500–5500 B.C.
  Munhata   ca. 6500–5000 B.C.
POTTERY   ca. 5000–4000 B.C.
  Jericho IX   ca. 5000–4500 B.C.
  Yarmukian (Sha'ar ha-Golan)   ca. 4500–4250 B.C.

CHALCOLITHIC AGE   ca. 4000–3300 B.C.

JERICHO VIII   ca. 4000–3600 B.C.

Bronze Age

Early ca. 33rd–21st centuries B.C.

Middle
    I ca. 21st–19th centuries B.C.
    II ca. 1850–1500 B.C.

Late
    I ca. 15th century B.C.
    II ca. 1400–1150 B.C.

Iron Age
    I ca. 12th–10th centuries B.C.
    II ca. late 10th–early 6th centuries B.C.
    III ca. early 6th century–332 B.C.

Hellenistic Period   332–63 B.C.

Roman Period   63 B.C.–A.D. 323

Nabataean Period   (main) 2nd century B.C.–2nd century A.D.

Byzantine Period   A.D. 323–636

BIBLIOGRAPHY: Albright, W. F., in Ehrich, R. W. (Ed.), *Chronologies in Old World Archaeology;* Amiran, Ruth, in *The Holy Land,* and *Antiquity and Survival,* II:2–3; Anati, E., *Palestine Before the Hebrews;* Garrod, D. A. E., Bate, D. M. A., *The Stone Age of Mount Carmel;* Kenyon, Kathleen M., *Archaeology in the Holy Land;* Stekelis, M., *Israel Exploration Journal,* 1, 1950–51; and Wright, G. E., *Shechem.*

Herod Chart

The Herodian Family

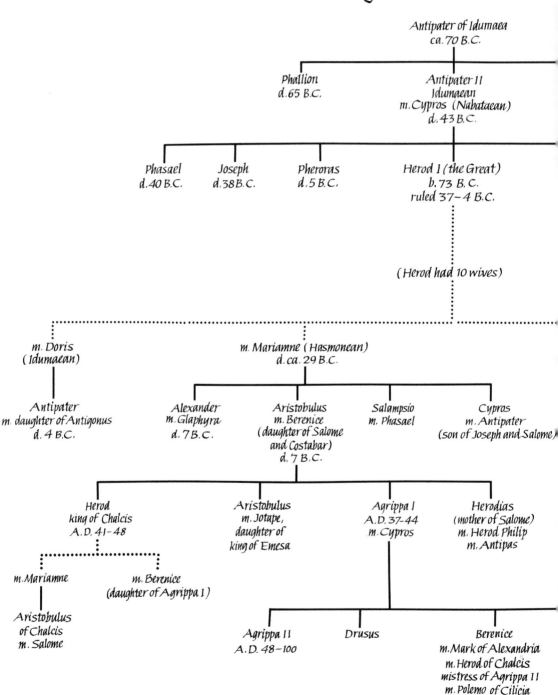

Antipater of Idumaea
ca. 70 B.C.

Phallion
d. 65 B.C.

Antipater II
Idumaean
m. Cypros (Nabataean)
d. 43 B.C.

Phasael
d. 40 B.C.

Joseph
d. 38 B.C.

Pheroras
d. 5 B.C.

Herod I (the Great)
b. 73 B.C.
ruled 37–4 B.C.

(Herod had 10 wives)

m. Doris
(Idumaean)

m. Mariamne (Hasmonean)
d. ca. 29 B.C.

Antipater
m. daughter of Antigonus
d. 4 B.C.

Alexander
m. Glaphyra
d. 7 B.C.

Aristobulus
m. Berenice
(daughter of Salome
and Costabar)
d. 7 B.C.

Salampsio
m. Phasael

Cypros
m. Antipater
(son of Joseph and Salome)

Herod
king of Chalcis
A.D. 41–48

Aristobulus
m. Jotape,
daughter of
king of Emesa

Agrippa I
A.D. 37–44
m. Cypros

Herodias
(mother of Salome)
m. Herod Philip
m. Antipas

m. Mariamne

m. Berenice
(daughter of Agrippa I)

Aristobulus
of Chalcis
m. Salome

Agrippa II
A.D. 48–100

Drusus

Berenice
m. Mark of Alexandria
m. Herod of Chalcis
mistress of Agrippa II
m. Polemo of Cilicia
mistress of Titus

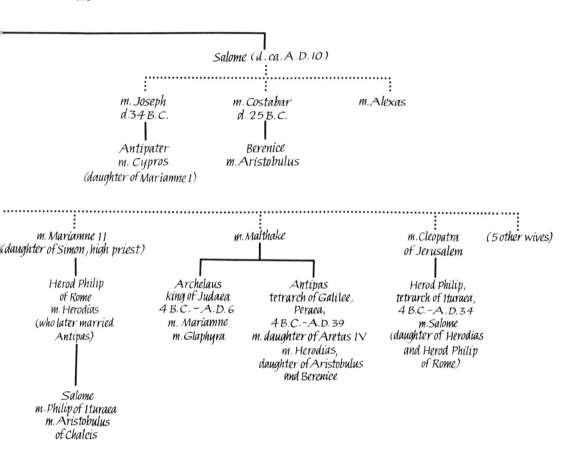

Joseph
m. Salome
d. 34 B.C.

Salome (d. ca. A.D. 10)

m. Joseph
d. 34 B.C.

m. Costabar
d. 25 B.C.

m. Alexas

Antipater
m. Cypros
(daughter of Mariamne I)

Berenice
m. Aristobulus

m. Mariamne II
(daughter of Simon, high priest)

m. Malthake

m. Cleopatra
of Jerusalem

(5 other wives)

Herod Philip
of Rome
m. Herodias
(who later married
Antipas)

Archelaus
king of Judaea
4 B.C. – A.D. 6
m. Mariamne
m. Glaphyra

Antipas
tetrarch of Galilee,
Peraea,
4 B.C.–A.D. 39
m. daughter of Aretas IV
m. Herodias,
daughter of Aristobulus
and Berenice

Herod Philip,
tetrarch of Ituraea,
4 B.C.–A.D. 34
m. Salome
(daughter of Herodias
and Herod Philip
of Rome)

Salome
m. Philip of Ituraea
m. Aristobulus
of Chalcis

Drusilla
m. Aziz of Emesa
m. Antonius Felix,
procurator of Judaea

Mariamne

(BIBLIOGRAPHY

The Life and Times of Herod the Great
and
The Later Herods,

Both by Stewart Perowne)

Indexes

General Index

226

Ptolemy, 192
Punon, 1, 2, 29, 84
Pylos, 9

Qalat er-Rabad, 63, 97
Qalat esh-Shaqif, 26
qanat, 169
Qasr el-Heir el-Gharbi, 90
qattarah, 79, 175
Qeseir Amra, 90
Qir-haresheth, 13
Qumran, 6, 103
Qurun Hattin, 43

Rabbath Ammon, 88, 92, 95
Racine, 32
Rahab, 175–179
Rameses II, 174
Ramoth-gilead, 139
Rashid Hamid, 82, 123, 124, 133
Rechabites, 85
Red Sea, 1, 2
Rehob, 170
Remeimin, 100
Rephaim, 88
reservoir, 9–11, 69
Reuben, 94
Rhodes, 187, 192
Rhodian jar handle, 187
Rig Veda, 8
Romans, 11, 16, 25, 31–34, 45, 99, 169

Sabhah, 91
Safadi, 151, 154
Saint George Monastery, 35, 64
Saint Mary Basilica, 90
Saladin, 43
Salome, 74, 192
salt, 2, 13, 22
Samaria, 29, 80
Samaritan, 6, 195
Samuel, 85
sarcophagus, 174
Satan, 35, 37
Saul, 95, 130, 131, 132, 133, 134, 174
Schliemann, Heinrich, 8
Schweig, S. J., iv, 51, 64

scrolls, 103
Scythopolis, 46, 99
Sea of Galilee, 20, 21, 23, 27, 33, 41, 44, 45, 52, 76
Sea of Lot, 19
Sea People, 6
Seat of Moses, 73
Sebastieh, 99, 192, 194
sedentary settlement, 12, 103–105
Seir, 113
Seleucids, 24, 188
Senir, 27
Septuagint, 188
serpent representation at Beth-shan, 173
Sethos I, 145
Sha'ar ha-Golan, 92, 148, 150, 182
Shabbath, 195
Sheikh Audeh ibn Jad, 83
sheninah, 97
Shibboleth, 108
Shiloh, 138
Shobek, 13
shofar, 47
Sidon, 192
Sihon, 88, 93, 106
Sirion, 27
sites, ancient, 17
skull, 20, 23, 161
Smith, G. A., 3, 43
snake pottery, 147
Sodom, 81
Solomon, 4, 25, 29, 32, 119, 184
Sparta, 192
springs, 9–10, 21, 44, 46
Stekelis, Moshe, 20, 92
stoa, 73
Strabo, 46–47
Succoth, 17, 93, 111, 113, 119, 120–125, 127
synagogue, 42, 47–48, 70–71, 73, 168
Syria, 2, 24, 38, 96

Tabaqat Fahil, 143
Tabun, 23
Tacitus, 31
Talmud, 44
tamarisk tree, 132

watchtower, 120–121
water, 9–11, 13, 67, 116, 169
weapons, 23
weather, 3
weaving, 24
wells, 9–11, 13
Winnett, F. V., 104
Wirgin, W., 73
Wright, G. E., 41

Yadin, Yigael, 40
Yangtze, 19
Yarmuk, 20, 45, 87–89, 92

Zacchaeus, 197
Zaphon, 93, 108, 109, 110, 122, 126, 142
Zarethan, 13, 17, 67, 93, 118, 119, 126, 127, 128, 129, 162, 163
Zedekiah, 184–185
Zeinati Arabs, 133, 134, 135, 136
Zeinati, Mohammed, 133–134
zibdeh, 97
ziqlab, 87
zodiac, 47, 48, 173
zoomorphic juglet, 155
zor, 20, 77–78, 117, 127

Index of Biblical Citations